OUT

OF THE

DEPTHS

A NOVEL BY

DANNY & WANDA PELFREY

For Freddie

Danny Pelfrey

Wanda Pelfrey

Xulon
PRESS

www.xulonpress.com

Prologue`

O n a windy March day in 1929 in the quiet little North Georgia town of Adairsville, the checker game in progress at Bowdoin's Drug Store pitted Warren Whitworth, the town undertaker, against his close friend Crisp Hambright. The participant's concentration disturbed a bit by the whistle of the 5:48 north bound locomotive speeding toward its destination of Chattanooga, sixty miles to the north; Warren took some time in making his move. "Are you going to play or just sit there?" Crisp chided the laid back, middle aged undertaker.

Joe Addington, one of several spectators, made a suggestion to Crisp. "You might be better off if he just sat there. He has you cornered."

Wick White, dressed in his usual overalls and plaid shirt hesitantly entered the store taking a spot behind the other spectators. Tom Noland, losing interest in the one-sided checker game, immediately noticed that the tanned, weather beaten face of the farmer to be uncharacteristically pale. "What's the matter, Wick? You see a ghost?"

"No, but I think I heard one," he shot back. His comment got the attention of everyone in the little drug store. "On my way home from the field, I heard what sounded to me like a baby crying somewhere in the Oothcaloga cemetery. When I got home my kids told me they heard it several times today. I thought you fellows might like to go with me to investigate."

Crisp, curious as well as recognizing that a suspended game could be the only way to avoid yet another embarrassing defeat at the hands of the cocky undertaker expressed agreement suggesting, "What are we waiting on? The noisy group, leaving the checker board behind, crowded into Warren's Buick. Joe Addington jumped on one running board with Wick on the other. The undertaker, ignoring the verbal digs about his driving skills, drove north on the Dixie Highway one mile out of town past Wick's place parking in front of Oothcaloga Baptist Church. The unlikely group of investigators climbed out of the car making their way up the hillside to the cemetery.

About halfway through the graveyard Wick stopped. A look of concentration on his face the tall gentleman called out, "Listen? You hear it?"

"It does sound like crying!" Crisp exclaimed motioning with a raised right hand for his companions to stop their chatter. After a moment of hesitation, Warren with the others lagging behind him ran toward a plot where he had only a couple of days previously interred an elderly woman. Upon reaching the grave, he fell to his knees and with his bare hands began digging away loose shale. He scraped away only a few inches of the red dirt when his fingers touched living flesh! Warren lifted an infant from its shallow grave as an astonished Joe Addington removed his own jacket wrapping it around the crying child.

With the stunned group quickly making their way back to their transportation, Warren continued to hold the cold and obviously hungry little girl to his chest. "Better head straight to Doc Bowdoin's place," Warren suggested. It was Crisp who got behind the wheel this time.

The excited friends, relieved to find Doc Bowdoin on duty in the big white Victorian house that was both his home and office, stormed the reception area. The dignified demeanor of the doctor who had long cared for the sick and afflicted of Adairsville was noticeably disturbed by seven overwrought gentlemen simultaneously explaining why they happened to have an only hours old infant in their possession. After piecing together enough of the conversation to figure out what was going on, Doc Bowdoin instructed Warren, "Bring her into the examining room. The rest of you will have to stay out here."

Returning minutes later, the doctor used a formal tone of voice to which his friends had grown accustomed to speak to the band of rescuers, "You gentlemen are to be commended. This little lass seems to be extremely healthy. She gives promise of a long life. Several factors saved her life in spite of being buried for who knows how many hours." He explained, "a piece of ruffle, probably torn from the mother's petticoat, protected her face; the loose shale no doubt, permitted the passage of sufficient air; and the umbilical cord was clogged with soft shale which prevented her from bleeding to death."

Doctor Bowdoin, returning to his examining room, bathed the little foundling and wrapped her in a blanket. Arrangements to care for the child were quickly made. Tom Noland, with the blessing of the other men, carried her to his wife who was nursing their six month old son. Shortly thereafter a compassionate Adairsville resident gave the baby the layette she had completed before miscarrying a few weeks earlier. The little castaway who was buried alive quickly became the talk of the town. The sheriff came from Cartersville, the county seat, to launch an investigation. A woman living near the cemetery reported seeing a girl at a distance early on the day the child was found. Someone else reported a young woman, whose identity was unknown, getting off the train the previous day and walking toward Oothcaloga Baptist Church. It was never determined if the two leads had anything to do with the strange events beside the Dixie highway near Adairsville.

No one remembered who originated the name, but to the people of Adairsville the tiny blue eyed beauty naturally became "Dixie Adair". Reverend Hawkins, once the pastor of the Adairsville Methodist Church, was now the superintendent of the Methodist Children's Home in Decatur, near Atlanta. Everyone involved agreed that Dixie Adair would be placed in the care of Rev. Hawkins. Arrangements were made and in quick order little Dixie became a city girl. In the weeks, months, and even years that followed many rumors about Dixie circulated through the town. It was said that a wealthy couple from one of the northern states adopted the lovely tot while she was still an infant. The rumors became more and more elaborate while Rev. Hawkins, no doubt, felt it was in the child's best interest to keep a shield of secrecy around her.

For a while the people in Adairsville and the surrounding area talked a lot about the strange incident. In time the rumors died down. Dixie Adair was almost forgotten by the citizens of the sleepy town nestled in the foothills of North Georgia. Who would have guessed that after more than ninety years Dixie would again disturb the tranquility of that peaceful village?

Chapter 1

For as long as he could remember, Davis Morgan had enjoyed the view of Adairsville he now observed from a top of what the locals called Cassville Mountain. A local columnist often described the tiny town as "his Norman Rockwell village." That is the way Davis, perhaps a bit influenced by blind nostalgia thought of the hamlet of less than 5000 residents.

Will Harben, a local writer, though one hundred years removed, once remarked that he wrote best about North Georgia and its people after being away for awhile. Davis knew what Harben was talking about. Absence has a way of reinforcing the good of a home town, while allowing the bad to fade from remembrance. Only a month earlier Davis returned to Adairsville after several years in Richmond, Virginia and more than fifteen in Indianapolis, Indiana. Influenced by the blue sky, the crisp air, and the greenness of all of nature coming alive on this late April afternoon, the temptation to take the old 41 route back to town, also known as the Dixie Highway and Peacock Alley, was too much for Davis. He knew that by taking the slightly longer route he was running the risk of arriving late for dinner with his daughter and her roommate, but he rationalized that if he were a few minutes late they would surely understand.

Going past Hambright's Lake, memories of Davis' childhood when his grandparents lived near the lake involuntarily flooded his mind. He resisted the urge to stop and stroll around the small body of water. It seemed in the month he had been back, the need to stroll and remember was constant. Dinner was waiting, so he kept his foot on the accelerator steering his five year old Ford toward town.

A lot of change had occurred in Davis' world over the past year. He returned home to Adairsville eleven months after Julie, his wife of nearly a quarter of a century, lost her fight with cancer. The beautiful Julie was his inspiration, his motivator, his best friend, as well as the love of his life. It was she who made life exciting, worthwhile, and fun. Davis smiled as he remembered a tongue in cheek statement of a close friend. "Morgan, you are the best example I know of a man who would never have amounted to a hill of beans had he not married the right girl." His friend did not know how right he was. After her death, Morgan sometimes tried to shut out his memories of Julie, thinking that would keep the pain away, but, how could he suppress memories of someone who was so much a part of his life? Often his recall of their years together still brought pain, but even in the midst of that pain he desperately needed to reminiscence about those special times.

Through the years, Davis had attained a degree of success as a pastor in both Virginia and Indiana, but Julie had not been gone long before he realized that any success he had in the ministry was closely tied to his partnership with her. Dealing with the pressures of trying to please hundreds of people—each with different expectations for their minister—was difficult for Davis even with Julie's encouragement. Without that encouragement it was practically impossible. Davis had long loved collecting books, and that was the direction he decided to take. He was no longer Pastor Davis Morgan. He was attempting to redirect his energy into the less stressful business of rare books. His new business cards identified him as Davis Morgan, bookman.

Davis, not sure how he felt about that at times still experienced more than a twinge of guilt about leaving what he long ago surmised to be his calling. On the other hand, he felt as if a thousand pounds had been lifted from his shoulders. Many friends had questioned the wisdom of his decision twenty-six years ago when he, a quiet, shy boy of eighteen, announced his intention to prepare for the pastorate. His immediate supervisor at the carpet mill where he worked that summer was one of them. "How will you ever be able to stand before people and speak? You fall apart every time I or any of the other supervisors approach you."

College and seminary preparation and later the work to which Davis had dedicated his life were rather difficult for him, even painful at times, but his high school sweetheart was there from the beginning providing whatever support he needed to get the job done. How could he possibly continue without her? During her last weeks of life Julie often asked him to read Psalm 30 to her. At the time he thought he was ministering to her.

Now he realized she had been preparing him for this time of transition. On his darkest days he echoed one of David's laments. *"Hear, O Lord, be merciful to me. O Lord, be my help."* [Psalm 30:10)

The car bounced as it went across the railroad track. Davis turned right driving a few hundred yards before turning left to pull into his driveway. He inherited the classic Victorian style house from his mother, her home for more than thirty-eight years before her death five years earlier. The big white dwelling with the wrap around porch was home for him during most of his childhood and his high school days. It was one of the constants in his life. Those two week summer vacations he, Julie, and their daughter, Amy, spent in the big house with his mother were some of the happiest days he experienced. The residence was divided into two apartments and rented after Davis' mother passed away. That arrangement still bothered him a bit, but had seemed the only logical thing to do at the time. Amy graduated from college, last May, landing a job teaching high school English in Adairsville. She, along with a roommate, Deidre Ross, also a teacher, moved into one of the apartments.

When plans were made to come home and open the Corra Harris Bookshop in the 1902 Stock Exchange just across the railroad from his boyhood address, it was a given that Davis would choose to live in the other apartment. It was an arrangement that pleased him, since he had the advantage of not only living in the place he loved as a boy, but he would also get to be near his daughter until she and Jay Archer would be married later in the year. If the book business proved successful, Davis hoped to restore the house to a single family residence once more. That was one of several goals he set for himself when he returned to the place of his birth.

Walking across the porch, Davis took his keys from his pocket, opened the front door immediately going to his answering machine to check for messages; a habit left over from his days in the ministry. *"Davis, this is Ed Hagan. I would appreciate it if you would drop by my house tonight? I have something extremely important to show you. Thanks."*

Ed Hagan, a reliable handy man with a sour disposition, had done some painting, repairs, cleaning and other work for Davis before the move back to Adairsville. Davis wondered what Ed had to show him. They were no more than casual acquaintances, and Davis at times found himself turned off by Ed's rather crude manner; however, he had proven to be a good worker. He made a mental note to go by Ed's home immediately after he had dinner with Amy and Deidre. Looking at his watch, Davis noticed it was a couple of minutes past six. He stepped into the bathroom to wash his hands. It seemed he always came back from book buying trips with dirty hands. He hurried out the front door to the porch and around the corner to the side entrance that led to Amy and Deidre's apartment.

He knocked. Deidre, his daughter's room mate, appeared. "Hi, Davis," she greeted him with a cheerful smile. "I think it's about ready." Davis was always conscious of his slightly expanding waistline and thinning hair in the presence of the trim twenty-eight year old brunette with the clear blue eyes and easy smile.

"Good, I'm just about starved," he responded.

"I bet you got so involved searching for books that you didn't bother to eat any lunch." Amy spoke from the kitchen where she was placing a full dish on the table.

"I guess you still know me better than anyone else," he laughed. "I got busy and lost track of time. It was three o'clock before I thought about a meal, and then I decided that to eat lunch at that time would spoil this fantastic dinner you ladies have prepared. A small package of potato chips and a diet coke have been my only nourishment since the two donuts and coffee I had for breakfast this morning."

"I hope your opinion doesn't change after you taste the roast," Amy said smiling. "After all we are known more for our beauty and intelligence than our cooking."

"You have never let me down before," he said. "I can't remember any of your meals that weren't absolutely delicious."

"You are just saying that because I'm your little girl," his petite offspring with short auburn hair replied. She walked over and kissed him on the cheek. "Besides, you better say it's good, or you will have to start eating somewhere else on Monday nights. Chips and donuts will get old quick if that is all you are having."

"Did you find any good books?" Deidre questioned.

"Let's go to the table before he answers that question," Amy suggested. "Dinner will be cold before we can eat it if he starts talking about books."

Davis was hungry, but it was difficult to determine which he enjoyed most, the roast, and potatoes or the conversation about his book buying trip to Atlanta. "It wasn't as profitable a trip as the one I made to Alabama last week," he said between bites. "I made the rounds to the thrift stores and found almost a full box of books I can price from eight to twenty-five dollars each. I didn't pay more than two dollars for any one volume, so I guess I did all right. I found some decent novels and the usual assortment of World War II and U.S histories. It's amazing how certain titles turn up again and again in the thrift stores. I found a nice first edition copy of Michener's, *The Bridge at Andau*, but unfortunately it's missing the dust jacket."

"That means it is worth only about twenty-five percent of what it would be worth with the jacket," Amy was proud to get the opportunity to impress her father with one of the few facts about book collecting she had picked up from him over the past few weeks.

"Very close," Davis said. "I'll probably price it at ten or twelve dollars, but with the jacket it would be worth at least fifty dollars."

"I don't understand that," Deidre responded. "Why does the presence of a dust jacket make the book worth so much more?"

"It isn't such a big deal if the volume is being bought simply to read, but collectors expect every book they buy to appear just as it did when it was issued," Davis explained. "Any thing published after 1960 needs to look almost perfect, and of course have a dust jacket in top notch condition to bring top price."

After dinner, Davis wanted to go back to his apartment, turn on his TV, lean back in his favorite chair and watch the Braves play the Chicago Cubs, but he knew he needed to go by Ed Hagan's house. Ed lived a couple of miles north of town past Oothcaloga Church and cemetery. He had better get started. The sooner he took care of this chore, the quicker he could get to the game. "I hate to eat and run," he said to the girls as he headed for the door, "but I've got things to do."

"It's your turn to wash the dishes next Monday," Amy jokingly told him. "In fact, I think you owe us a couple of nights of washing and clean up." She knew that loading the dish washer and scrubbing pots and pans were among his least favorite chores. It was a reaction to his job as a college freshman to clean up the school kitchen after dinner each evening. He often joked that he was the only guy on campus with dishpan hands in those days.

"I think I am busy next Monday night after dinner," Davis teased. "But I'll see what I can do." It was dark by the time Davis reached Ed's place, a small bungalow sitting a considerable distance off the highway. Seeing light in the house, he got out of the car and headed for the door. Only a few houses stood in view from Ed's yard, the closest being a good two hundred yards away; yet it seemed to Davis that all of Ed's neighbors had at least three dogs and they were competing to see which could bark the loudest and longest.

A car, appearing to be a late model Lexus, sped from behind the house as Davis approached the front door. It swerved to barely miss his old Ford. The security light on a pole beside the driveway enabled him to see that two people were in the front seat. He didn't recognize the car nor did he get a good enough view of the passengers to recognize them, though neither appeared to be Ed. Whoever they were, he decided, they didn't need to be on the road. Probably needed a designated driver he reasoned.

Ed isn't much of a house keeper. Davis observed the sad state of the front room visible through the small window on the door as he rang the door bell. *Maybe it's not Ed's house keeping! Maybe the room has been trashed!* That thought nagged at him in light of the speeding visitors he had just seen leaving. "Ed, are you in there?" After knocking and calling out for Ed again, he sensed that all was not right and reluctantly turned the knob. The unlocked door opened. He reluctantly took a step into the living room and again cried, "Ed, its Davis Morgan. Are you at home?"

Walking slowly through the wrecked living room into the dining room and kitchen Davis discovered they were in no better shape than the front room. Cabinet doors were wide open and plates and glasses were broken, leaving glass on the counters and floor. Drawers were pulled out with their former contents scattered. "*Nobody could be this bad at housekeeping,*" Davis thought to himself.

Now starting to panic, Davis headed to a bedroom which he found in as much disarray as the other rooms. "Ed, you here?" he asked, not really expecting an answer. Moving into the narrow hallway that separated the two bedrooms, he saw light shining in what was obviously the bathroom. He hesitated before walking toward the open door. He was gripped by an eerie feeling that made him weak in the knees. He thought he expected the worst, but nothing could have prepared him for the hideous sight in the small room.

Chapter 2

————◆✕◆————

F rozen in the doorway of the small room Davis was unable to believe what he was seeing. Thinking he was going to be sick, he covered his mouth with his left hand. He once was the first person to arrive at an automobile accident scene where two people had been killed, but the trauma he had witnessed then had not come close in comparison to what he was now seeing. The body of a man, presumably Ed Hagan, lay face down over the edge of the bathtub. His hands, behind him, taped together with duct tape. His head was a bloody mass. Blood was splattered everywhere in the small room.

Running back into the bedroom, Davis reached for his cell phone, but quickly realized he had left it on his kitchen table. Not really knowing why other than it is the way they do it at murder scenes on T. V., he took out his handkerchief using it to pick up the receiver of the phone he had noticed on his way through. He punched 911. "This is Davis Morgan. You had better get someone out to Ed Hagan's house north of town on the old Dixie highway. I think Ed's been murdered!"

In a daze, Davis didn't fully comprehend what the person on the other end of the line said, but he was confident he had given her enough information to enable her to get someone there immediately. He almost ran through the living room on his way to the front entrance where he waited for someone to arrive. He fought the nausea that was threatening to overwhelm him. He heard the siren of the police car moments before it arrived. The ambulance with lights flashing was not far behind. "What's the problem here?" The young police officer, he recognized as Charley Nelson, asked getting out of the passenger side of the patrol car. "Hey, you had better sit down on those steps. You don't look so good." He seemed concerned motioning toward the steps.

"When you see what's in that house, you're not going to look so good either," Davis shot back to the young officer who happened to be the younger brother of one of his high school team mates and long time friend. "You had better check the bathroom."

The two officers went inside without further comment. Moments later they returned telling the ambulance attendants there was nothing they could do but deliver the body when the time came. It proved to be a long and trying evening for Davis. He answered questions for the two officers plus the county sheriff and one of his deputies. Davis continued to be in a fog asking himself several times if all this was real.

Both Amy and Deidre were seated in their cozy living quarters with magazines in hand. "Your Dad seems to be doing well since getting settled," Deidre remarked.

"Not bad. He at least is putting up a good front, but I can tell he still hasn't dealt with losing Mom. I see a lot of sadness in his eyes. They were probably as close as any two people who have ever lived. They did almost everything together."

"I was a little concerned when you told me he was going to be living next door. I am not sure what I was expecting, but I am certain it wasn't what he turned out to be. He is a really neat guy, not at all like most of the preachers I've known."

"I guess Dad has always been somewhat of a contradiction. He is warm but extremely shy, strict but loving, educated but down to earth, fun loving but some times a little straight laced. He is strong but easy to manipulate. I remember learning in a college lit class about the difference between 'flat' characters and 'dynamic' ones. 'Flat' characters are generally stereotypes. They are good or bad, industrious or good for nothing, not much crossover. Such characters are easy to grasp, but usually pretty boring. A 'dynamic' character; on the other hand, is often complex and sometimes contradictory, neither entirely good nor entirely bad. He may be completely reliable in one area and totally inadequate in another. It is the 'dynamic' character that is the heart of good literature. If Dad were a character in a book he would be a 'dynamic' character, but then I am slightly biased. I love my Dad."

"Well, I feel good about having him next door. What about Jay?" Deidre asked laughing. "Is he a 'flat' or 'dynamic' character?"

"Definitely dynamic," Amy announced without hesitation.

"Do you think you might be a little biased there also?"

"Maybe a little," Amy admitted.

On that note I think I am going to go to my bedroom and review the material for tomorrow's first class. I never feel as if I am totally prepared for that particular group. Then I need to turn in early so I can get up in the morning for my quiet time. That is something I have been neglecting and I miss it."

"I'm not very sleepy. I think I am going to read for a while longer." Sitting alone with her bridal magazine Amy, as often had been the case in past months, had a feeling of thankfulness that she and Deidre had found each other. Deidre's encouragement played a major role in getting her through the loss of her mother. Dealing with the aftermath of that awful tragedy while being separated from her father had been an ordeal, and she would forever be grateful to her friend for providing a shoulder on which to cry. Deidre was always ready to listen when she needed to vent, but she also knew to back off when time alone was needed. When diversions were called for, she provided them. She seemed always to know just what to say or do. That is not to suggest there had not been tension at times. There were moments when Deidre seemed to lose patience with her, but even those sessions usually turned out for good. Amy, an only child, decided this must be what it is like to have a big sister.

One of Amy's regrets was that during the months she was struggling with her own loss, she offered almost no support to Deidre who was also hurting. That oversight was partly due to her obsession with her own personal problems, but also had to do with her roommate's failure to confide in her. Perhaps under the circumstances her friend did not want to burden her with her own troubles or maybe she just didn't want to talk about it. Deidre tended to be a rather private person. By piecing together information gathered in various conversations Amy learned that Deidre's plans for her own wedding had crumbled just days before the event was to take place when she discovered that Jeff, her fiancé, had been involved with several other women. The breakup had occurred not long before she and Deidre became acquainted and agreed to be roommates, yet Amy had heard very little of Jeff.

Sirens interrupted Amy's thoughts, which was not unusual since they were located only a little more than a half mile from the fire department and less than that from the police station. Sirens were a regular part of their lives. After an hour or so, realizing her father had not returned home, Amy tried to reach him on his cell phone without success. Considering the sirens she was a little concerned and stayed up longer than she should listening for the sound of her dad's car.

After what seemed to Davis like an eternity, the sheriff gave him permission to leave. "I don't think we need you for anything else. We'll have to stay around until the boys from the county lab finish up. You can go on home. We have your number if we need you. Do you want my deputy to drive you?" The sheriff offered very much aware of Davis' shaken condition.

"I can make it home on my own," Davis assured the sheriff. He was surprised to see lights still on in Amy and Deidre's apartment when he pulled into his driveway. It was well past their normal bed time. He knew he would need to face Amy. He did not know what he would tell her. The last thing he wanted to do was to frighten her. By the time he got to the porch she was coming through the door to meet him.

"I heard sirens earlier and knowing you were still out I couldn't sleep. Do you know what happened?"

"I'm afraid I do," he told her. "I was right in the middle of the whole mess. I found Ed Hagan shot to death at his home. It has been one of the worst nights of my life." By this time his daughter had made her way to him, putting her arms around his neck she held him as tightly as she could. The embrace helped to calm his nerves a bit and allowed him to get his thoughts together.

Davis walked with Amy into her apartment knowing he would need to give her more information. Deidre, obviously awakened by the commotion, appeared in the living room with a puzzled look on her face. He managed to tell them about the incident without including too many details. After a half hour or so, he said good night, told them to make sure they locked the deadbolt behind him informing them they could call if there were any problems. This was one time Davis wished Amy didn't have a roommate. He would have felt better having her with him where he could watch her closely. *At least she is under the same roof*, he thought.

After taking a long shower, Davis went to bed. Sleep did not come easy. Several times during the night he tried to pray, but praying had been difficult for him over the past months and, even in the midst of such a crisis, conversation with the Lord was not coming easy. Verse 8 of Psalm 30 floated through his subconscious. "*To you, O Lord, I called; I cried for mercy.*" The sleep he did get was interrupted often by strange dreams he was glad he could not remember when morning came.

Chapter 3

————◆✕◆————

J oining the guys at the Little Rock Café for breakfast would not be a good idea, Davis decided. Eating breakfast with several old friends who had local businesses or jobs with flexibility had been a bright spot for him since he had been back in Adairsville, but this morning he didn't feel like answering the questions that were sure to be asked of him about what happened at Ed Hagan's place. News travels fast in a small town like Adairsville. The guys would already know about the murder and they would know that he found the victim. They would quiz him from the time he walked through the door. He did not feel up to such an interrogation.

Taking a cup of coffee and a stale donut he found in the kitchen cabinet, Davis headed to work. Often he walked, but for some reason he felt it important to have a car nearby today, so he drove the short distance across the railroad to the south end of the business section where his shop was located in the largest of the fifteen or so buildings abutting one another making up the "downtown" business area. The little frame white Methodist Church built in the 19th century, along with its annex constructed in more recent years, stood at the other end of the block near the Adairsville Inn, a restaurant popular with people throughout the North Georgia region. When Davis was a child there was grass and big oak trees in the area between the street in front of the stores and the railroad; however, the park had long since given way to asphalt. Everyone in town now bemoaned that decision, but the politicians at the time argued that you had to make way for progress. Parking was needed.

Most of the structures on the, public square, as many referred to it even though it is not technically a square, were built before 1900. As the story goes several of them were designed and constructed by a man named Schmitz, a German who had been with Sherman on his destructive march through Georgia. After the war, the young builder returned to the state he helped burn to the ground in order to do his part to reconstruct it. His work still stands all over town. Many of the Victorian homes, such as the one in which Davis now lives, can still be identified as a Schmitz home by his stained glass window trademark located somewhere in the house.

The building now known as the 1902 Stock Exchange was one of the last projects of the beloved builder before his death. It was first a general store, but through the years had been remodeled serving as everything from a furniture store to a movie theater. Before being bought by the current owners, it had been divided into three sections on the main floor. Each section housed a different business. The upper floor had not been used, except by pigeons, in decades until recently. The new owners, inspired by the potential of the edifice and its location, invested major dollars in restoring it. The main floor was remodeled to house antiques and gifts, a quality luncheon area that might best be described as a tea room, and now the Corra Harris Bookshop, named for a local writer who was the wife of a Methodist preacher and author of *The Circuit Riders Wife* as well as sixteen other books published in the early twentieth century. A beautiful spiral staircase leads upstairs, where there is now a gorgeous dinner theater complete with antique chandeliers and period furnishings.

The location, two miles off Interstate seventy-five, exactly half-way between Atlanta and Chattanooga, is almost perfect. Combine that with Barnsley Gardens, a nearby attraction that pulls in the tour buses, the popular Adairsville Inn, and the quaintness of the town, and the possibilities are endless.

Having such a setting for the bookshop was definitely an advantage. The location would provide traffic. The arrangement worked well for Davis. He made more sales when he was there to help potential customers find what they were looking for, but he was not required to be in his shop since the mall clerk was available for purchases. That gave him opportunity to search for stock which was his favorite aspect of the business. He recently told someone who questioned his new occupation, "I'm in the business because I like to buy books." He was joking, but there was a lot of truth in that statement. Davis found it hard to explain to most people the satisfaction he found in discovering valuable editions of books in the most unlikely places such as the scarce first edition copy of Harper Lee's *To Kill*

A Mockingbird he had uncovered in a box of books he purchased recently in Alabama.

The ability to be away from the shop also enabled Davis to pursue other interests. Only last week, he wrote his first, "As I Remember It" column for the North Bartow News. He looked forward to developing the many column ideas he had about local people and events from Adairsville's past. Davis also had the idea that he would like to create mystery stories. He had gotten a taste of writing while doing articles for Christian journals, even writing an inspirational book for a Denver publisher. Davis often joked that a few of his closest friends and only a handful of others had read the book, but he; nevertheless, was bitten by the writing bug, and now that he had time, would like to pursue that interest.

Davis poured himself a cup of coffee. The tea room only opened for lunch, but Janie, the perky hard working mall clerk, made sure there was always coffee for those laboring in the building. He sat down in a chair in the corner where he kept his computer. Paying for internet connection at the Stock Exchange added to his monthly expenses, but made his time there much more productive. He listed many books on eBay each week and sold most of the ones he listed. It took time because every item must be described in detail including its condition as well as the condition of the dust jacket. The book must be scanned and its picture uploaded to the description. Often questions from potential buyers had to be answered, and, of course, when a sale was completed there was wrapping and mailing. The internet had vastly changed the collectible book business in the past few years. Quaint bookshops were still appealing and wonderful, but in these days anyone needing to make a living with books had to learn to use the internet. Even with the internet, all but the most successful booksellers often had to supplement with additional income.

"I hear you had a real *terrifying* experience last night." Janie spoke as she briskly walked past the table where he was seated.

"You are right about that. I'm not sure the word terrifying does the experience justice. It's a night I'll never forget." He continued to work without looking up hoping she would take the hint and drop the subject.

"When I get a little time you are going to have to tell me about it."

A sound like a grunt came from Davis' mouth while he continued his efforts at the computer. Business usually was not brisk on Tuesday, and this one was no exception. Davis sold an inexpensive Georgia history and a fist edition of one of Michener's early titles. He got a sandwich from the tea room at lunch time. After devouring it, he decided to walk down the street to stretch his legs a bit. He passed the antique store about half way down the street which was housed in the building that had once been his mother's florist shop. He wished the owner would keep the store in better shape. His mother, whom everyone knew as "Miss Elaine" had started working there when she came to town to live with the Walsh family after she was orphaned as a teenager. Most everyone in Adairsville knew her and almost all agreed with Davis that she was a very special lady.

"Miss Ross, would you please come to the office." Deidre, who was lecturing her Junior American history class on the period between the War of 1812 and the War Between the States, was surprised to hear the summons from the school receptionist coming through the intercom system. She gave her class work instructions before she left them in the care of Emma, the student teacher she had been pleased to have assisting her over the past six weeks.

"You have a visitor Miss Ross," the smiling middle aged secretary told her as she glanced toward a six foot tall thirty-something blond young man who nervously smiled at Deidre when she turned in his direction. She was at a loss as to how to respond when she saw Jeff, her former fiancé.

Jeff with a nervous smile on his face spoke first. "Hi Deidre, I need to talk with you and did not know how to find you other than at school. I hope my interruption will not cause you any problems."

Seeing Jeff standing there as if nothing had happened caused Deidre to feel both anger and delight. Without a greeting of any kind, she responded, "We can't talk here Jeff. I'll meet you at McDonalds out by the interstate as soon as school is dismissed at three forty-five."

"That will be great. I sure have missed you," he added as they walked out into the hall way.

"What are you doing here?" Deidre's voice revealed aggravation. "I don't know what we could possibly have to talk about."

"Don't be angry with me sweetheart. You are the most important person in my life."

"Don't Jeff. I thought I had made it clear that it is over."

"It's not over for me. I'll see you at the restaurant in a couple of hours." He spoke as he turned his back toward her hurriedly walking away as if he was afraid she would cancel their meeting if he stayed any longer.

The knot in Deidre's stomach seemed to grow larger during the two hours she waited for school to be dismissed. It had been almost a year since seeing Jeff. That last session together had been anything but pleasant. Arriving at the fast food restaurant she found Jeff seated at a table in a corner away from the few customers who were there at that time of the day. He had already retrieved coffee for both of them. That was typical of Jeff, charming and thoughtful. *I think his charm may be his worst enemy,* Deidre decided as she was seated in the chair that Jeff pulled from under the table for her.

"It is so good to see you. I can't get you off my mind, sweetheart." Jeff didn't waste any time getting into his reason for being there. "I still love you Deidre and I want you in my life."

"I have never doubted that you want me in your life, but is there room for me there with all the other women?" She questioned as she took a sip of coffee.

"That's not fair. Those women meant absolutely nothing to me other than a good time. I promise you it will never happen again. I will be a one-woman man from this day on if you will come back to me."

"Jeff, there is nothing you can say that will convince me that you can be trusted. Your first marriage ended because of your unfaithfulness. You were unfaithful to me and I suspect to every other woman you have seriously dated. I think you will always be looking for a good time. When I consider your track record I wonder if you are capable of committing to only one woman. We don't need to trudge through all this again."

"There have been some changes Deidre. I have accepted a job, a good job in St. Louis that will pay me more money than I ever thought possible. I will be relocating there in three weeks. I want you to go with me. We can be married whenever you wish. I know we could be good together."

"I hope the job has not been the only change Jeff. I wish you only happiness in the future, but that future will not include me. I've told you that before."

Jeff's tone changed, "Is there someone else?" he abruptly asked.

"No Jeff, there is no one else. It is my desire that there will be someone someday. And that is my wish for you, that you will find someone who will make you happy. I know now that I am not that person."

They talked for twenty-five minutes more, but mostly the remainder of the conversation was nothing more than small talk, mainly exchange of information about mutual friends. When Jeff got up to leave he told Deidre, "If you should change your mind, you know where to reach me, at least for the next three weeks. All offers are off the table after those three weeks are up," he warned.

"Have a good life Jeff." Deidre smiled sadly speaking from her heart as she too got up and turned toward the door. Outside Jeff kissed her cheek and got in his car and she in hers. Sitting under the wheel she watched Jeff drive to the ramp and turn toward Atlanta. She knew she would likely never see him again and because of that she felt a deep sadness. Combined with the desire to cry was a feeling of relief. As hard as it was, she knew she had done the right thing. For the first time she felt there was closure.

Charley Nelson, a female dispatcher, and the mayor, Sam Ellison were mulling around the office when Davis stopped by the police station. "Have you made any progress in finding Ed's murderer?" Davis directed his question to Charley.

"We don't know much more now than we knew last night," the young officer replied.

"If you ask me it was a case of plain old robbery gone badly." The mayor spoke up as he walked toward the door. "That's why everything was such a mess."

After the mayor left the room Charley lowered his voice. "I think that's just wishful thinking. The major may be a good administrator, but he is not much of a detective. There were valuables left all over the house. It is true you probably scared the murderers away, but I feel sure there would have been more things missing if robbery was the motive. Besides, the killing was execution style, probably done by a professional."

"That's scary. You don't expect professional hit men to be operating in Adairsville."

"You're right. It's been years since we have had anything like this. Oh, occasionally someone is killed in a domestic squabble or by someone trying to get money to buy drugs, but, as a rule, this sort of thing doesn't feel like an Adairsville crime. After having some time to think about it, I don't suppose you have any guesses as to what Ed wanted to show you?" Charley questioned.

"I don't have the slightest idea," Davis told him. "I have thought about it constantly and nothing comes to mind."

"That might be a key to solving the case. Maybe whoever murdered him was looking for whatever he was planning to show you."

"That is an interesting theory, but what would a career handyman have to show a former preacher turned bookseller that would bring professional killers down on him?"

"That's a good question. If I knew the answer, maybe I could solve the case and get to be chief or at least get a raise," the young officer laughed.

"You may be chief someday, but whether you ever get a raise, considering the tightness of our city counsel, that's another matter," Davis joked.

"By the way, I enjoyed your column in last week's paper," Charley commented. "My brother; on the other hand, took exception to it."

"Sure he did," Davis laughed. "He and I were on that football team that suffered the 57-0 defeat that for some strange reason no one in town remembers but me."

"Well, we got a laugh out of it. I think the best part was ribbing Dean."

"You tell him I told you about Coach Allison taking him out of the game to protect him from serious injury. That will really rile him up."

"I know he'll like hearing that. There is one other thing I want to ask you about," said Charlie. He again lowered his voice looking around for potential eavesdroppers. Tell me about your daughter's pretty roommate. I know Amy is engaged, but I haven't heard that her roommate is seeing anyone."

"Even if my daughter weren't engaged, I would forbid her to date a skirt chasing playboy like you." Davis smiled at the young policeman as he spoke. "Deidre is several years older than Amy. She taught for three years in the Atlanta area before moving here at the start of this school year. I believe she is originally from South Georgia, Valdosta I think. She was for a time engaged to a guy from Atlanta, but I guess he hurt her pretty badly. She doesn't seem anxious to jump back into a serious relationship. She is a sweet girl, and please don't forget, if you do ask her out, you will have to answer to me if you are anything other than the perfect gentleman." Davis' comment was only half in jest. Charley knew that by his tone as well as the expression on his face.

"I'll take that under consideration," Charlie told him with a grin.

"Let me know if you come up with anything else on the case. I need to get back to the shop."

Chapter 4

All afternoon Davis dreaded going to the funeral home on Wednesday night. Viewing hours were something he had not enjoyed during his years of ministry. As a pastor he spent many miserable hours in chapels, parlors or mortuaries through the years. It had always seemed to him that the tradition put families through unnecessary stress as did several other funeral customs. He decided when he left the ministry that this was something he would pass on now that he had a choice, but when seven o'clock p.m. came, Davis was on his way to the mortuary where Ed's family would be receiving friends. As much as he disliked the tradition it was a matter of obligation and respect.

The imposing big white house serving as funeral home with chapel attached sits off the road on the highest point in Adairsville maybe one hundred fifty yards behind the 1902 Stock Exchange. Memories and bits of local history flashed through Davis' mind as he entered the historical structure that pre-dated the Civil War. He smiled and shook the hand while briefly speaking to the gray headed man in the dark suit and red tie stationed at the door. He knew he was suppose to know the older gentleman, but could not recall his name. Surprisingly, a fairly large crowd had gathered. Davis reasoned that Ed's work skills had probably made him at least a casual acquaintance with a large portion of the populace, but he sadly realized the circumstances of his death most likely inflated the number of those in attendance. Curiosity, perhaps, accounted for the relatively large crowd.

Not knowing any of Ed's family, Davis introduced himself to a lady in a black dress standing near the coffin in which Ed's body was displayed guessing she was a family member. She explained that she was Nona, Ed's sister from Athens. "We have a brother who still lives in Alabama, but

I don't think he is going to be able to make it. He is in bad health. Besides we have not been a close family for a long time." She pointed out Ed's former wife not having a great deal of good to say about her. Not wanting to stand silently alone, Davis introduced himself to the former Mrs. Hagan. Her name was Alice, and she didn't seem to him to be too broken up over Ed's demise.

After accepting Davis' awkward expression of sympathy, the widow pointed to an attractive blond in a black dress. "Isn't that Tracie Ennis?" The blond lady looked his way, smiled, and then hurried toward him. He was taken by surprise when she threw her arms around him and hugged him tightly. It wasn't until that moment that Davis realized that Tracie Ennis was Traci Stevens: cheerleader, homecoming queen, and every boy's dream during his high school years.

"I don't think I've seen you since your graduation." Tracie's voice gave away her excitement. "You still look like you could play a little football and basketball," she said stepping back and looking at him from head to toe. "Where have you been for the past twenty-six years?"

"Mostly I've been in Indiana." Davis' surprise had almost left him speechless. He quickly regained his composure saying the first thing that came to his mind. "Tracie, you look great!" Not original, but at least he didn't make a fool of himself.

"I heard you were the one who found Ed. Until yesterday, I didn't know you were back in town." Much of the remaining time at the funeral home was spent getting reacquainted with the beautiful Tracie Ennis or Stevens or whoever she was now. He learned that after two years at the University of Georgia, she married a young man who inherited a large trucking company in Cincinnati. Five years ago her husband had died in an accident. She returned to Adairsville, two and a half years back building a house on Boyd Mountain three miles west of town. Being the best handy man in town Ed Hagan had often done yard work and odd jobs for her.

Walking to the parking lot, Tracie promised Davis she would stop by his shop some time in the near future. "I want you to teach me the ins and outs of book collecting," she told him.

"Stop by around noon just about any day other than Monday or Sunday, and I'll buy you lunch," he suggested.

"It's a date," the beautiful lady said with a twinkle in her eyes. She opened the door of a classy red sports car that Davis who considered automobiles only transportation, could not identify. She turned stepping back toward him. "Davis it really is good to see you again." Much to his delight she kissed him on the cheek before returning to her car. Even reflecting upon the fact that he had fallen into the trap of socializing at visitation, Davis drove home in a better mood than any time over the past couple of days.

On Thursday morning Charley Nelson stopped by the Corra Harris Bookshop finding Davis at one of the tables in the tea room drinking a cup of coffee. Davis much preferred Janie's coffee to his own. "I think we found the car you saw leaving Ed's place," the young policeman told Davis. "We found a black Lexus abandoned on an old logging road in the woods about two miles west of Kingston. Turns out it was a rental from an agency located at the Atlanta Airport."

"If those guys were professional hit men, they no doubt, rented the vehicle when they arrived from Chicago, New York, or wherever such low life comes from," Davis speculated. "I suppose the names and identification they used when they rented the car were phony?"

"I am sure that is the case. One would reason that professional hit men would never leave such obvious clues, but we are following up on the information we got from the agency. Who knows, perhaps they fouled up and left us a lead. You are a lucky man Davis. I suspect the killers abandoned the rental because they thought you could I.D. it. For all they knew, you were able to get the license number. It's a wonder they didn't stop, tape your hands behind you and kill you like they did Ed."

"I can't say that hasn't crossed my mind. I guess they would be relieved to find out that with my limited knowledge of automobiles I was lucky to recognize that it was a Lexus! Do you think the fact the car was abandoned near here rather than in Atlanta somewhere is an indication they are still around?"

"It's possible. It is also possible that someone locally is involved since one would think a third party had to pick them up when they abandoned their ride."

"Who in Adairsville would hire hit men to murder Ed and why?"

"I don't know," Charley shrugged. "But I doubt too many people outside Adairsville knew Ed! Don't tell him I told you, but the chief believes it could be Alice, Ed's ex. Seems there have been a lot of hard feelings brought on by fighting over property since the divorce. A large percentage of all murders are domestically related, but it just doesn't feel that way to me."

"I met her last night at the funeral home. While she certainly didn't seem to fit the description of a grieving widow, I can't see her master-minding a murder," agreed Davis.

"By the way, I understand there is a guy in town calling himself "Mr. Brown" who is asking a lot of questions about our local history. He was at the library and newspaper office. He talked to our illustrious mayor yesterday. Sam told him you might have some material on our town's past in your bookstore. Have you seen anything of him?"

"There was a middle aged gentleman by just before closing time yesterday who wanted to know if I had letters, diaries, legal documents, newspapers or anything of that nature that would be dated around 1929. I couldn't help him much. He had a lot of questions, but I didn't learn anything about him. He didn't even give me a name though I did recognize his accent as being New England. Do you think he had anything to do with Ed's murder?"

Charley simply said, "See you," as he walked toward the door.

The remainder of the week was spent doing the kind of boring activities book sellers must do to pay the bills. Davis cleaned and priced, listed auctions on eBay, and spent the better part of one afternoon in nearby Rome appraising a library a college professor recently inherited from an uncle. The crates were packed with mostly classics with many being nicely bound editions. Indiana history was also a common theme since the library had originated in that state. Some of the most valuable volumes were the scarce county histories. There were, to Davis' delight, a couple of Hemingway first editions and one by Steinbeck. Being impressed with the condition of all three volumes Davis made Dr. Bray, the owner, a good offer for the three first editions as well as an early set of Poe's works bound in leather, but was immediately turned down. The Professor was a little like a child with a whole room full of new toys. He was pleasantly surprised when he was handed the itemized value sheet totaling over thirteen thousand dollars which would serve as a basis for insuring the handsome library.

After completing the appraisal Davis stopped at a steak house for dinner where he read the current Atlanta Journal-Constitution while eating his meal. Being alone in restaurants was one of the little difficulties Davis discovered when Julie was no longer with him. For some reason he had found that a newspaper made the meal slightly more tolerable. After the big dinner he told himself he needed to cut back to take off ten or fifteen pounds.

Darkness had fallen before Davis left Rome. Instead of selecting the most traveled route back home, he decided on old highway fifty-three. He noticed in his rear view mirror headlights continually staying several car lengths behind him. When he speeded up the car behind him speeded up. He slowed down, and it slowed down. He turned off old fifty-three onto Rush Chapel Road and the vehicle behind him also made the right turn. When the road dead ended into highway one-forty he made a right toward Adairsville. The driver behind him did the same. He was convinced he was being followed.

Remembering that his old high school friend Dean Nelson, Charley's brother, lived just ahead on the right. Davis turned into the graveled driveway. His "friend" behind him stopped on the side of the road, maybe two hundred feet before getting to the drive. The lights beside the front door came on as Dean, all six foot five and two hundred eighty pounds of him, stepped outside. Davis immediately heard the suspicious automobile speed away.

"Just thought I'd stop and say hello. How is that beautiful wife of yours doing?" Davis greeted his old friend Dean. Not wanting Dean to think he was paranoid, Davis did not mention he believed he was being followed. After spending thirty minutes talking about old times, he was on his way again, probably leaving Dean and Sherrie a bit perplexed. *I know it's my imagination*, Davis tried to convince himself yet glancing behind him in the midst of those thoughts. *There is no reason for those guys to come back to harm me. I'm sure there is a logical explanation for whatever that driver was doing.* He arrived home without further incident.

On Sunday Davis drove Amy and Deidre up the hill to the little church in which he had grown up, both girls had considered it their home church since coming to town. Now after all these years, it was again *his* church. Amy, an accomplished organist and pianist, played the organ for the congregation's traditional service to which the older members clung tightly. Even though Davis thoroughly enjoyed the traditional hymns, he understood the need for a more blended service designed to draw more young families to the historic church. He knew that wasn't likely to happen any time soon at the church on the hill. Davis sat with Deidre on the hard pew. *I think I know now why I sometimes had such a hard time holding people's attention*; he thought when the seat became uncomfortable. He was glad when they stood to sing *How Great Thou Art*. After Tom Johnson's rather eloquent prayer they were seated again. Davis was very much aware of how little space there was between him and Deidre. The scent of her perfume filled his nostrils as he tried unsuccessfully to forget that she was next to him. *I hope Tracie stops by the shop this week*, he thought, feeling a bit guilty. Then his mind made a mad dash to Julie.

John Redmond, the gentle young giant with the red hair and broad smile, in the pulpit immediately got Davis' attention. "There is nothing you can do that will cause God to stop loving you! You can separate yourself from Him! You can rebel against him, you can even actively engage in battle against Him, but He will not stop loving you, not under any circumstances."

The youthful preacher, beginning a new series of sermons from the little New Testament book of Titus, explained why he felt Titus was left in Crete to minister even when he was discouraged evidently preferring to go elsewhere. "Titus was instructed to stay in Crete because God loved the people of Crete. It wasn't that they necessarily deserved that love. Some of the citizens of that city were not very nice people. Paul writes in Titus 1:12, "Even one of their own prophets has said, 'Cretans are always liars, evil brutes, lazy gluttons.' But God is love. He loves us even when we do not deserve to be loved. That is called grace. One of the reasons for Titus remaining among a people such as those in Crete was God's grace. God left Titus there because he loved the people in that part of the world. Aren't you glad for the grace of God? Aren't you glad God has chosen to give us what we need rather than what we deserve?" Maintaining eye contact with his congregation, the preacher quoted the last stanza of a beloved old hymn:

> Could we with ink the ocean fill?
> And were the skies of parchment made,
> Were every blade of grass a quill,
> And every man a scribe by trade,

To write the love of God above,
Would drain the ocean dry,
Nor could the scroll contain the whole,
Though stretched from sky to sky.

Davis continued to listen as the obviously well prepared speaker effectively pointed out that Titus was also left in Crete because God loved *him*.

"...God is more concerned about our character than our comfort," John reminded his attentive congregation. 'A smooth sea never made a good sailor'. Titus needed to stay in Crete if he would become an effective servant. For his own sake he needed some adversity in his life. Davis listened closely as the preacher quoted James 1:2-4:

> Consider it pure joy, my brothers, whenever you face trials of many kinds, because you know that the testing of your faith develops perseverance. Perseverance must finish its work so that you may be mature and complete, not lacking anything.

The preacher summarized. "We need to endure the storms of life to make us strong and more effective."

The sermon was thought provoking temporarily reassuring Davis. He needed to be reminded of God's love for him, but at the same time he felt guilty that he had not "remained in Crete." "That was a great message!" Davis complimented the young preacher on the way out. "I love your preaching. It is Biblical, practical and easy to follow. Not a lot of men your age have so quickly gotten to the level you have attained as a communicator."

"That is a real compliment coming from someone with your experience and talent," the young preacher responded. "You better be careful. You might give me the big head."

After the service Davis dropped his daughter and her room mate off at their apartment where they would quickly change to meet friends traveling to Chattanooga for an afternoon concert. Davis went to a nearby restaurant where he ate meat loaf while reading his newspaper. He felt even more alone than usual. The afternoon was spent in his recliner reading, napping and watching the baseball game on TV, a day quite different from his busy Sunday afternoons during his years in the ministry. He remained inside all afternoon missing the constant activity of his past.

Two men sat in a vehicle parked in a lot across the street and railroad tracks from the big house on Railroad Street. On this Sunday afternoon there were no other cars in the lot. A high powered rifle lay under the feet of the man sitting on the passenger side. They were waiting for Davis Morgan to come outside to his porch or front yard. It would take only seconds for the sharp shooter to open the car door, step outside, take aim, pull the trigger and get back into the car. He had done it before in other cities. They would be on their way before anyone knew what happened. The two men waited for more than two hours, but Morgan never showed.

When an elderly lady came out of her house, located just a hundred fifty feet from where they were parked, to sit in the chair on her front porch the driver started the engine. They drove away. The man on the passenger side remarked, "We'll get him another day."

Since the Stock Exchange closed on Mondays, Davis usually searched for stock on that day. This Monday was no exception. He made the rounds in Chattanooga. Known as "The Scenic City of the South," the medium sized city was a favorite of Davis'. Even though it was for him about the same distance as to Atlanta, he could get across the Tennessee line and to Chattanooga fifteen minutes quicker due to less traffic. Look Out Mountain, Ruby Falls, Rock City and several historic Civil War battlefields were just a few of the sites to be enjoyed when one took in what this area offered, but today he needed to stick to business. Davis was able to make several good buys. He had befriended a junk dealer there a month earlier when he first came back to Adairsville. The gentleman had absolutely no interest in books. He often bought estates for resale at auction, but now saved any books among the items he purchased for Davis. It meant taking many titles he would not be able to sell, but he would donate those later to the Salvation Army or Goodwill store. Davis was afraid if he did not accept all items his friend had for him, he would not be offered future lots. Who knew what would be in those boxes. On this day Davis gave the friendly business man an envelope with a one hundred dollar bill in it explaining that he sold several of the books he received on his last trip for a good deal more than expected. Davis figured it was only fair. It kept his conscience clear considering the small amount the congenial gentleman required him to pay.

Today's trip to the large cluttered building resulted in a number of good, not exceptional, but good Civil War titles. Davis always got excited about discovering Civil War material at a price that enabled him to make a decent profit. Such books were almost always over priced. Everyone seemed to be convinced that any thing about the Civil War is valuable. The boxed two volume set of The Tragic Years 1860-1865 by Angel and Miers that was in today's stack was of special interest to Davis. First edition and in excellent condition, this find would surely bring forty dollars or more. There were probably ten or twelve other titles that would sell for fifteen to thirty dollars each.

As he started south toward interstate 75 Davis' mood was upbeat. He knew the Chattanooga Lookouts, the AA minor league team, was playing Jackson Mississippi in a day game. The last four or five innings would be left in the game. As a long time baseball fan, he was tempted to stop when he passed the ball park, but decided he needed to get home. He did not want to be late for his standing Monday night date with Amy and Deidre. Monday night was fast becoming his favorite night of the week, but he was sorely disappointed when he arrived discovering that Deidre was in a meeting and absent from her usual Monday night place around the table. His mood improved somewhat when the young woman arrived a half hour after he and Amy had finished their meals sitting down with them to visit for a few minutes.

Chapter 5

Tracie Ennis was true to her promise. At a little past twelve-thirty she and Davis walked down the street to the Inn where she ordered a salad and he a chicken sandwich for lunch. "I don't mind telling you I had a big crush on you when you were a senior," she told Davis. "Of course, I wasn't alone. You being the strong, silent football and basketball star, every girl in the sophomore class, and I suspect the junior and senior classes as well felt the same way."

"That's flattering, though I suspect a little overstated," Davis told her. "As you know we were a small high school. I guess it was like being a big fish in a small pond."

"Nevertheless, you were a special athlete as well as a person, and we all knew it. I bet half the girls in our high school were heart broken when you started going steady with Julie. But that was then and this is now. Maybe I'll get a second chance," she giggled.

Davis thought he felt his heart speed up a bit. Could this gorgeous lady, who looked at least ten years younger than she had to be, actually be interested in him? She could have her pick of available men. Why would she choose him? And Davis got the impression that she would definitely do the choosing. Allowing herself to be chosen would not be Tracie Ennis' style.

Davis recalled something so small and insignificant from his senior year that he guessed almost any normal person would not have remembered it past the night it occurred. It was toward the end of a basketball game in Dalton in which he was having one of the best games in his high school career. The ball went out of bounds touched last by the opposition. He stood out of bounds a few feet from where the cheerleaders were doing their thing. As he took the ball from the official ready to pass it in bounds to a teammate, he heard the voice of the pretty sophomore, Tracie Stevens, above all the other noise in the gym. "Let's go Davis honey," she screamed, then repeated the words of encouragement.

It was her use of the word "honey" that had caused Davis to feel a little bit the way he was feeling now, over twenty-five years later, sitting across the table from her. After finishing their meal, they walked back to the shop with Davis very much aware of her touch as she held his left arm. He was also conscience of the stares of those they passed on the sidewalk.

"Which is your most valuable book?" Tracie asked after they were back in the shop.

Walking behind the glass display case, Davis pushed the case door toward the middle and removed a beautiful green book. This is a first edition, first issue, copy of Charles Dickens' Hard Times, For These Times. "You'll notice it is inscribed by Dickens." He carefully turned to the inscription on the endpaper.

"You mean that is actually Charles Dickens' signature?" she excitedly asked.

"You bet,"

"How do you know it is a first edition?"

"Well, it's green cloth. It's dated 1854, published by Brandburn and Evans in London and notice," he said pointing to the lower portion of the spine, "The price, five shillings, is stamped here. These are what we call points. The points must be in evidence in order for this book to be a first." Davis was pleased for the opportunity to demonstrate to Traci his knowledge of collectible books.

"Where did you get such a rare item?" she asked.

"I got this one at an auction in Indianapolis before I left there. I cannot afford many high end purchases, but I wanted one as a show piece."

"How much are you asking for this one?" Tracie held the object with both hands and looked at it almost reverently.

"Since it is a first edition in almost perfect condition inscribed by Dickens, I can get at least eight thousand dollars for it."

"Sold!" Tracie quickly responded taking Davis by surprise.

"Are you sure? That is a lot of money!"

"I can afford it," she assured him.

"In that case, take it to Janie, and she will receive your check."

Tracie took Davis' right hand with her left and moving her face toward him, gently pecked him on the cheek. "Call me soon," she suggested as she picked up one of his business cards off the top of the display case writing a telephone number on back handing it to him.

"I will," Davis told her. "You can count on it."

Ten minutes after she had gone, Davis was still floating on air. He didn't know if it was because he made an eight thousand dollar sale or because he was strongly attracted to this beautiful creature who dressed like a model, drove an expensive sports car, and spent thousands of dollars on an impulsive whim. He had never known anyone like her. He took the card with her telephone number written on back, looking at it as if he could not believe it was actually in his possession before he carefully placed it in his wallet which he placed back in his hip pocket. With a grin on his face he softly muttered, "You'd better believe I'm going to call you soon. *At least now I can afford to date her,* he reasoned. He realized that there was a thought nagging at his subconscious. Tracie had carefully steered clear of spiritual subjects during their time together. What's more, Davis knew he had not tried very hard to redirect the conversations.

Telephone," Janie shouted to him across the room. "Charley Nelson wants to talk with you. Are you in some kind of trouble with the law? It would be a shame to be arrested after making that big sale." She laughed as she gave him the phone.

"Hello, Charley. What's up?"

"I need your help. Last night a neighbor spotted someone trying to get into Ed Hagan's house. She didn't get a good look, but she could see a flash light moving about. She called us immediately. We drove out to take a look, but evidently scared him or them off. As we approached the front door we heard noise in the bushes behind the house. By the time we got to the back, whoever it was had disappeared into the woods."

"Do you think it was the same guys who killed Ed?"

"I think it is possible that you scared them off the night they killed Ed before they found what they were looking for. I suspect they returned last night to continue the search. On the other hand, it could have been curious kids. Last night's prowlers may have nothing whatsoever to do with the murder."

"But if they are the killers, evidently whatever they are looking for is important enough for them to chance a return to the crime scene." Davis' summation caused him to think he had probably been reading too many detective stories.

"I doubt they had enough time to do much searching last night. Whatever they are looking for is probably still in the house. I wondered if you might go out there with me. Ed wanted you to see something. We searched time and time again, but I thought you might recognize whatever Ed thought would interest you."

"Sure I would be happy to go with you. Want to do it right now?"

"If it's a good time for you, there's no time like the present. I'll be there in a couple of minutes."

When they got out of the patrol car at the small five room cottage, Davis tried to hide his apprehension from Charley. He did not expect anything to happen in broad daylight, after all he was there with a police officer; however, the memories of his last visit brought him an uneasy feeling. There seemed to him to be a stillness hovering over the place. He dreaded going inside. Charley, ever the observant police officer, turned to Davis as they walked toward the door. He spoke in an effort to reassure him, "I know exactly how you feel. It's not easy, is it?"

"Let's get it done," Davis suggested picking up his pace. The words had hardly gotten out of his mouth when Davis heard a loud noise that seemed to come from every direction. It was almost as if some super-human power had picked him up and hurled him backward. He hit the ground hard with the back of his head banging against something. He was finding it hard to breathe. When he opened his eyes, flames seemed to be everywhere!

Chapter 6

━━━━━◆✕◆━━━━━

Lying on the ground, Davis was for a moment too stunned to move and incapable of any rational thought. After what seemed like forever, but probably wasn't more than a few seconds, he was able to get in a position where he was resting on his hands and knees like some four-legged creature. It was then that he noticed Charley flat on his back fifteen feet to his right. Davis, with extra effort, finally got to his feet staggering toward Charley. He remembered that an injured person was not supposed to be moved, but aware of the intense heat coming from the flames in front of him, Davis took both of Charley's upper arms and dragged him backwards away from the burning house. "Are you okay?" He asked though still dazed from the explosion. There was no answer. "Charley, are you alright?" He cried out close to panic. He could hear sirens in the distance, probably just starting the three or four minute journey to the burning house. He saw a neighbor lady running across the field toward him. In his dazed condition it looked to him as if she was running in slow motion.

The fire truck and the concerned runner arrived about the same time. The last thing Davis remembered before awakening in the emergency section of the hospital in Rome was seeing a fireman kneeling over Charley.

"Dad, how are you feeling?" Davis heard Amy's voice and looked up to see her standing over him. Deidre was behind her. "You sure gave us a scare." Amy took his hand.

After a few moments of consciousness, he remembered the circumstances that brought him there. "How is Charley?" He immediately questioned the two young ladies.

"I haven't heard. I need to tell the nurse that you are conscious. I'll see what I can find out about Charley."

When Amy left the small room Deidra stepped close to the bed and took the hand that Amy moments before had held. Her touch coupled with that beautiful smile made him glad the explosion had not ended his life. "I appreciate you being here." He looked up into her blue eyes, before closing his own.

Davis lay on his back, eyes closed until a doctor followed by a nurse came into the room. "It is about time you woke up," the doctor said to him. "You had a rather extensive nap."

"How long was I out?" Davis asked him.

"They tell me well over an hour," he answered. "We are going to admit you so we can get you checked out."

Amy returned to his bedside with good news. "Dean's wife told me Charley doesn't seem to have any serious injuries. He is rather banged up though."

"Thank God, I thought we had seen the last of Charley Nelson." Davis breathed a sigh of relief that his friend had survived the blast. Throughout the next day Davis endured a lot of punching and probing as the medical people tried to determine if there were hidden injuries. The first night after his close call, he found it difficult to sleep because soreness kept him from finding a comfortable position. He had only a mild concussion, but head injuries required caution.

The following morning the medical professionals kept him busy, but in the early afternoon, he walked down the hall to Charley's room. Charley, like himself, was bruised, scratched, and scorched, but doing well. He hardly got into the room before Charley started apologizing. "I never should have taken you out there!" he declared. "I should have known better. You could have been killed, and it would have been my fault."

"Don't worry about it; we are both still very much alive. That's what matters. You are not to blame. You didn't force me to go. You made the suggestion and I agreed."

"The EMTs told me you pulled me away from the fire. Thanks! I owe you one."

"You don't owe me anything. Have you talked with anyone about what caused the explosion?"

"The chief came by this morning. The Georgia Bureau of Investation is now involved. He said they are still combing the site, but it appeared to be an elaborate homemade bomb with some kind of timing devise, placed under the house. It could have been placed there the night before or shortly before we arrived. It is anyone's guess as to whether someone was trying to kill us or just destroy the house. If they were interested only in demolishing the house, then we happened to be at the wrong place at the wrong time."

"It isn't likely they were after us, is it?" Davis picked up the conversation. "Besides Janie and anyone who was at the station when you called, no one would have known we were going to the murder site."

"The chief and the mayor heard my conversation with you, but if anyone was trying to do us harm, they would have had to already had the bomb made, gotten to the house before us, planted it and exited. That is possible I guess, but not likely. My guess is they were trying to destroy whatever they had not found. We just happened to be there at the wrong time. If we had been one minute earlier we would have been in the middle of that explosion. Neither of us would be alive today. But what were they trying to eliminate? We probably would be well on our way to solving this case if we knew the answer to that question. The chief is insisting I take a few days off. I didn't put up much of a fight, because the time off will give me time to work on this without taking time out to write traffic tickets and handle school crossings. Even with the sheriff's department and the GBI on the case, I've got a personal stake in this." Charley spoke with a note of irritation in his voice.

"I know you are a good cop, but you better be careful," Davis warned. "Whoever these boys are, they are playing for keeps."

Later in the afternoon, Tracie strolled into his room looking like a model straight out of a fashion magazine. Dressed in a short sleeve tan blouse and light brown skirt with shoes that perfectly complimented her outfit, Davis thought he had never known anyone as physically beautiful as Tracie. "I came over as soon as I heard what happened," she explained. Looking at the burn on his arm she remarked, "They tell me you have no serious injuries, but that burn sure doesn't look good."

"It looks worst than it is. Caution is my only reason for still being here. They just want to be sure there are no hidden injuries. The doctors are driving me crazy with all their x-rays and tests, but they have found no real problems." He smiled at the beautiful lady with the short blond hair and little girl dimples. "I think they will release me in the morning after I see the doctor."

"I am relieved to hear that. You and that young cop are lucky to be alive.

"I don't see it as luck at all", Davis declared emphatically. "I believe the Lord was watching over us."

Tracie ignored his statement. "Do the police know who is responsible?"

"Not as far as I know."

"I heard the noise all the way up on the mountain, but I thought it was just a big blast at the quarry. Then I heard the news on the radio a little while ago. You should have had someone call me earlier," she scolded.

"Sorry. I guess Amy and I have been a little distracted. What did the newscasters say?" he asked.

"Only that there had been an explosion at the site of last week's murder and you along with a police officer were injured, but listed in satisfactory condition." Amy and Deidre arrived a few minutes later, having gotten away from school earlier than usual in order to visit him. He introduced the two young ladies to Tracie with the usual pleasantries being exchanged.

After Tracie left the room, Amy looked at her dad with a twinkle in her eyes. "So that is the Tracie you haven't been able to stop talking about since last week. I think you need to cool it. I don't want a stepmother who is so much more beautiful than I am."

"You don't have anything to worry about. There is no one more beautiful than you," he assured her with fatherly pride as he took her hand and kissed it.

Deidre said little during their stay in Davis' room. The two young teachers visited with Charley Nelson before returning home deciding he must be physically fine since he spend most of the twenty minutes they were in his room good naturedly hitting on both of them. After two nights as a patient in the hospital, Davis returned to his routine, but his actions were controlled by a new caution. Somebody might want him dead, but who and for what reason? He could think of none. He had to agree with Charley that the key to the whole thing might be in whatever it was that Ed wanted him to see, but no amount of mental investigation brought the slightest clue to what that was.

"We missed you the past few days," Janie told Davis as she gave him a warm hug.

"I bet you did. With no one around to make your life miserable, you were probably bored out of your mind," he teased the vivacious clerk. It was good to be back in his shop. Police chief Jim Hanson stopped by to ask him a few questions assuring him they would be patrolling his house regularly. Fearing for Amy and Deidre's safety, he was glad for that news and thanked the chief for the extra protection.

Later in the day Davis sat down to write his next, "As I Remember It" column. He had been thinking about a column about his mother. His biggest task in writing on that subject would be to filter all the material available to him. He would approach it by emphasizing her unselfishness. "Miss Elaine", as she was known by everyone in town, lived for others. She had been orphaned in her early teens, coming to Adairsville to live with John and Mary Walsh. From the beginning of her life in Adairsville, Davis' mom had been a fixture in the Walsh's florist shop. She loved flowers and learning to arrange them was easy and fun for her. John Walsh who had come to Adairsville from the west as a dry goods salesman met Mary, a local preacher's daughter, and decided to stay. He and his young bride opened a florist business. Elaine became the daughter they never had. Even though there was no blood relation Davis always considered John and Mary his grandparents.

His mother remained single much longer than was the norm in her day, but eventually married Jack Morgan shortly after her thirty-first birthday. Jack was several years older than she. Davis was born in the third year of their marriage. He was the only child the Morgan's had, perhaps because they had married so late in life. Davis could only slightly remember his father who died of an apparent heart attack when Davis was only five years old. John Walsh passed away in his early sixties while Mary lived a long life retiring from the florist business shortly after his death. For many years she was taken care of by Davis' mother as she went through one illness after another growing frailer with each.

"Miss Elaine" became sole proprietor of the family business keeping Adairsville beautiful with her arrangements until her death. Davis would be eternally grateful for his mother who more than any other single person molded his life. He owed much to Julie. Julie kept him on the right track. "Miss Elaine"; however, was the one who initially put him there. Words came easy to Davis as he wrote with a pencil on a yellow legal pad. He would transfer his column to laptop tonight and tomorrow deliver to the newspaper office by email the finished product simply entitled "Miss Elaine."

Thinking about his mother always produced mixed emotions. Remembering her brought joy, but even after all these years he still felt deprived now that she was no longer with him. These thoughts of love and loss pushed his mind to Julie. He desperately missed her. He wished he could talk with her about everything that had happened over the past two weeks. Together they would be able to sort it out. Without her, he felt like an incomplete person. He left the bookstore with a feeling of being a bit lost. Psalm 30: 7 floated to the top of his mind. "*O Lord, when you favored me you made my mountain stand firm, but when you hid your face I was dismayed.*" He went home to a dinner consisting of a ham sandwich and a diet coke with a few chips and an evening of listening to music while reading a mystery novel which was often interrupted by thoughts of what used to be. Julie filled his thoughts for much of the evening. He went to bed early, but sleep did not come easy. Tomorrow, he reasoned, he would get on top of things again.

Chapter 7

C alling Tracie, Davis suggested they spend Saturday together at Barnsley Gardens. "Janie can take care of things at the shop," he told her. "A beautiful spring day is forecast, and I would like to spend some time outside."

Tracie eagerly accepted the date. "I have wanted to see what they have done with the old place. I can think of no one I would rather see it with." Tracie gave him directions to her newly built house.

On Saturday morning Davis, in a much better frame of mind than he had been in recently, drove the three miles up the mountain west of town. It was one of those late spring days when the sky is blue and the birds seem to be happier than usual. He had not traveled this narrow country road since being back in Adairsville. What he saw when he arrived at his destination took him totally by surprise. He knew Tracie had received a rather substantial inheritance from her late husband's estate, but he was not prepared for the huge stone English Tudor style house that dominated the hillside above what he remembered from his childhood as a pasture where cows and horses grazed. As he drove the approximately three hundred fifty feet tree lined driveway from the main road to the regal structure, it occurred to him that he might be in over his head. Half expecting a butler in tails or a maid in uniform to answer the door, Davis pushed the door bell button, but it was a smiling Tracie who greeted him. "Well, how do you like my humble abode?" She questioned Davis with a smile as he stood with his mouth open in absolute awe.

He muttered a greeting and approval of her new home after which Tracie offered him a tour of the ground floor. "You don't want to see the rooms upstairs. My decorator is still working on them, but every thing down here is done, at least for now." More than impressed by all that he saw, it was the roomy library-study that really caught Davis' attention. He liked the antique library table he guessed was twelve feet long near the center of the room, but what really impressed him was the large oak bookcases that completely covered one wall from floor to ceiling that were completely lined with at least five hundred Easton Press books. Davis had once heard someone appropriately refer to the colorful leather bound Easton published books as the Rolls Royce of books. Tracie noticed his obvious interest in the beautiful leather bound volumes. She explained, "My decorator purchased those through eBay. They are mostly classic literature and history, but the main thing is they really dress up the room."

It always bothered Davis for people to consider books only decorative pieces, but his mind was so centered on the large colorful collection on the shelves that he missed the last part of Tracie's statement. Having a fair idea of what such books sold for on eBay, Davis quickly did the math in his mind. *There is almost twenty thousand dollars in books on those shelves,* He decided. They walked through a back door into the meticulously landscaped back yard where Tracie showed him the swimming pool which he decided was larger than the public pool in which he swam in his youth. The pool house was obviously more spacious than most of the places in which he and his family had lived during his years of ministry.

Ten minutes later opening the passenger door of his five year old Ford for Tracie made Davis a little self-conscience. *I wish I had at least washed it,* he thought as he noticed the clutter in the back seat when he closed the door. As they made their way down the mountain away from Tracie's estate turning south toward Kingston he began to regain some of his confidence. Barnsley Gardens was familiar to Davis from his years of growing up in Adairsville. In his teen years it was an old spooky estate in terribly run down condition to which he paid little attention. Since then he had picked up bits and pieces of its interesting history.

In the 1830s Godfrey Barnsley, a shipping tycoon from Savannah came to North Georgia with two friends. Each of the wealthy gentlemen bought several thousand acres on which they began developing working plantations. Barnsley was warned by the Cherokees in the area before the infamous removal called "the trail of tears" that the place where he chose to build his house was cursed. Despite that warning the confident business man who had always done things his way went ahead with his plans to build a beautiful Italian style villa distinctively different from the columned mansions usually found on Georgia plantations.

Barnsley called his plantation Woodlands. He brought flowers, plants, trees, and shrubs from all over the world for his gardens. He also brought back furniture from the various ports his ships visited. Before the main house could be completed, Barnsley's wife died. Davis never believed in ghost, but those who have worked at the resort through the years have reported that on some moonlit nights her shadowy image can still be seen roaming the gardens. True or not, it adds to the mystic of the charming resort. For a time after his wife's death, the wealthy shipper lost interest in completing the main house causing the work to be halted. Later it was resumed, but before completion, the Civil War erupted and Barnsley's fortune was lost. The house was abandoned some years later after a tornado did severe damage to the roof.

Tragedy after tragedy is part of the plantation's fascinating story. On one occasion a mad young prize fighter took the life of his brother on the premises, just one of a number of sad events to occur on the beautiful grounds. In the 1980s a wealthy foreign investor, who Davis had heard referred to as a Prince, purchased the property spending millions of dollars restoring the gardens, turning it into a popular resort and tourist spot complete with museum, gift shop, a four star restaurant, Inn, and championship caliber golf course.

Having not visited Barnsley Gardens since coming back to Adairsville, Davis was intrigued by what he found. Tracie was fascinated with the exotic flowers and bushes. Davis, being a student of history, particularly enjoyed the museum. He found a newspaper article displayed on the museum wall of special interest to him. The writer of the article, probably written in the 1930s, presented his view that Augusta Evans Wilson wrote the widely read post Civil War novel, *St. Elmo*, with Barnsley Gardens as the setting. It was pointed out in the piece that she was a guest at the plantation before she wrote the book. The writer offered the argument that many of the events described in the story were similar to ones that occurred in and around Adairsville while she was there. "I've never heard of *St. Elmo*," Tracie admitted while looking at the framed newspaper pages.

St. Elmo was the most widely published American novel before *Gone With The Wind*, Davis explained. "It was never acclaimed by the critics, but a favorite of the American people," he told her. "Its author, Augusta

Evans Wilson, spent the better part of her childhood living near Columbus, Georgia. Her adult life was spent in Mobile, Alabama. Chattanooga Tennessee also claims her. There is a suburb of that city that bears the name "*St. Elmo*".

"Being with you is definitely good for me intellectually. I learn all kinds of new facts when I hang around with you," Tracie exclaimed with a smile.

"The display of this article explains why so many people who have visited Barnsley Gardens come into my shop looking for St Elmo."

"Do you have a copy now?"

"I have two or three good reprint copies, no first or anything of particular value."

"Will you hold one of them for me?" She requested.

"Sure I will, but by today's standards, you will not find it easy reading."

"I just want it as a memento of our day together," she told him.

Before leaving the resort, Davis and Tracie had a late lunch at the restaurant. "This is great food. We're going to have to come here often," Tracie suggested. "I have had a wonderful time today."

"It has been a special day for me too. How about going to the dinner theater with me next Friday night at the Stock Exchange?" Davis was now feeling pretty confident in his relationship with Tracie. "A production of Louisa May Alcott's *Little Women* will be playing for the next three weekends. It should be fun."

"I will look forward to it." Tracie smiled sweetly reaching across the table to take his hand.

"Mrs. Ennis!" The male voice came from behind them.

Davis turned looking up at the owner of the voice, remembering him as the person who came into his shop looking for early Adairsville records. Mr. Brown, Charley had called him.

"I still need to talk with you as soon as possible."

"Now is not a good time." Tracie's mood changed drastically.

"Is there a time and place when I could meet with you? I would be happy to meet when-ever and wherever it's convenient for you. Just name it!"

"Call me tomorrow and we will work something out." She spoke rather sternly.

"I'll call you tomorrow morning. Have a nice day." He smiled, nodded to Davis and slowly walked back to the table where he was seated alone.

"Who is that man?" Davis asked.

"Oh, he is just someone who needs to talk with me about some business, nothing to be concerned about." Tracie matter-of-factly dismissed the subject as they returned to their meal. The sun was starting to go down in the west when Davis finally dropped the lovely lady off at the front door of her elaborate home. It had been an enjoyable day enabling Davis to block out some of the unpleasant events that had recently occurred. He hoped there would be many other days with the beautiful Tracie in his future.

That same evening, Charley Nelson called Davis to tell him that he had been questioning area motel clerks attempting to find any suspicious characters who had prolonged stays. "There are evidently some pretty strange characters getting off interstate 75 to spend the night in Adairsville, but so far none of them appear to be relevant to our situation. They are usually one night stays. I really haven't found anything that would be helpful to us," he reported. "If our bad guys are staying in an area motel, it must be in Rome, Calhoun or Cartersville. We will eventually get to those."

"I appreciate you keeping me posted. Tell me, what else do you know about this Mr. Brown who has been asking all the questions around town?"

"Why do you ask? Have you had any more contact with him?"

"Tracie and I spoke briefly with him at Barnsley Gardens earlier today."

"We learned that he is a private investigator from Boston. That's all we know about him. He probably doesn't have anything to do with Ed's murder or the bombing."

"You don't have any idea why he is here or why he is asking all the questions?" Davis inquired.

"No, we don't. He is probably working for a law firm on some sort of legal dispute. We were told that is the kind of thing he usually does."

"Thank you for the information. I appreciate your helpfulness," Davis told him. "You had better be careful. I've sort of gotten use to having you around. I wouldn't want you to get hurt. If anything should happen to you I would have no one to keep me informed."

"Thanks a lot Davis, and I thought you were concerned about me because I am such a lovable person. I'll be in touch."

Charley was alone in his apartment with no plans for the evening and nothing distressed him more than that situation. He had called several young ladies trying to set up a date, but none of them were available or anxious to go out for the evening on such short notice. He had even called a couple of friends to see if they wanted to get together and do something. He hated watching T.V. unless there was a good sporting event being telecast, but he cared little for baseball and that was the only game being shown tonight. Football or maybe a good Southeastern Conference college basketball game was more to his liking, but it was the wrong season for that.

His thoughts went to his work which he thoroughly enjoyed. For almost as long as Charley could remember he had wanted to be nothing but a cop. He knew about cars so his brother Dean wanted to bring him into his auto repair business. He appeased his brother for a couple of years by working with him, but he really didn't enjoy that kind of work. Dean was the oldest of the four brothers while Charley was the youngest who had come along accidentally almost ten years after the third. He idolized his older brother who could easily have played college and perhaps pro football had he stuck with it. Dean had the size and agility. After high school his brother spent only a few weeks at Clemson on scholarship before returning to Adairsville due to home sickness and perhaps a little love sickness as well. He and Sherrie had married not much more than a year out of high school. The garage business had been a good fit for Dean, but it wasn't what Charley wanted to spend the rest of his life doing. The two brothers were as different as day and night. Physically, Dean was like their Dad, standing almost six and a half feet tall, weighing in at around two seventy-five. Charley, on the other hand, was closer to five foot ten and less than one seventy-five. They were different in ways other than size. While Dean was a home body, Charley loved the night life. Charley sought excitement while Dean enjoyed a quiet restful evening. Dean was a devout family man while Charley had no plans to marry anyone any time soon. He was committed to playing the field, at least for the foreseeable future.

Charley remembered well their dad who passed away when his youngest son was nine years old. Howard Nelson, their father known by most of his friends as simply Chief, had for years been the single member of the Adairsville police department. It wasn't until the town started growing after Chief's death that a real force was put together. Charley had always wanted to follow in his father's footsteps. That dream had become a reality a little over a year ago. There was an opening which prompted his resume the very day the opening occurred. Charley was added to the force after pleading his case to the chief almost daily for a month. Chief Hanson had not regretted the decision. Charley quickly rose to be his right hand man. It was no secret to anyone that knew Charley that his ambition was to someday be chief and most of them figured he would achieve that dream in the not too distant future. The chief had already started talking about retirement. In the Adairsville department seniority was not the number one consideration for promotion. Charley lived, ate, and slept police work.

Charley knew that this thing involving his friend Davis was an opportunity for him to prove himself. Finding Ed Hagan's murderer would certainly be a feather in his cap or better yet a stripe on his sleeve. Thus far he had not had much luck, but he understood that if he latched onto it like a bull dog, his break would come. Good police work was just good old fashioned hard work. Charley had always believed a good policeman made his own breaks.

On Sunday morning Davis, Amy and Deidre attended a large church that Davis had wanted to visit in Kennesaw, since it was on their way to the Atlanta airport where they would pick up Jay Archer, Amy's fiancé. Jay, who Amy had met when they were both college students, had taken an engineering job with a large well respected company in Orlando, Florida. They decided they would use the few days Jay had off to get together to make wedding plans. Davis agreed to let him have his extra bedroom while in town. A decision he was not entirely comfortably with; nevertheless, the right thing to do, he decided. Jay was a fine enough young man, but Davis always found him rather boring. The only thing they seemed to have in common was Amy. When he and Jay were together, Jay wanted to talk about business and computers, while he was more interested in books, history, and people. *It won't be so bad,* he thought. *He will be with Amy most of the time.*

On the return trip, Davis drove Amy's car with Deidre on the passenger side. Jay and Amy sat in the back seat. It was a pleasant drive. Atlanta traffic on Sundays is nothing like it is on weekdays. They stopped for dinner at a Cracker Barrel Restaurant north of Marietta. The food was good and the conversation spirited. Even Jay contributed to the light hearted discussion about their antics while in college. *I'm going to give a tongue lashing to either of those girls who asks Jay about business,* he thought. On the other hand, he was delighted when Deidre asked, "Have you bought any interesting books lately? He could not resist telling them about the first edition copy of a book he purchased recently. "I bought it for a dollar. It's worth at least $100.00."

"Isn't that unethical?" Jay asked.

Davis suddenly remembered why Jay was such a pain.

"Shouldn't you give people more than a dollar or two for their valuable belongings?"

"If someone brings a collectable to me, I will tell them its value. If it is one I want, one that is marketable, I will give them up to 40% of its retail value; however, if I find a book in a thrift store, antique mall, or anywhere else I will simply pay the asking price regardless of the value. There is nothing unethical about that. It is just good business." Davis spoke more sharply than he intended.

"Okay," Jay responded in a tone that caused Davis to believe he was not convinced.

When they returned home, Deidre surprised Davis. "After all that food, I need to take a stroll. Would you like to join me?"

Davis was flattered until it occurred to him that she was trying to give Jay and Amy some time alone. "Sure, I could use some exercise myself," he answered.

Wedding on his mind, Davis said, "I know Amy is going to miss having her mom around while she plans her wedding. I am glad she has you to share her plans."

Deidre smiled a little sadly. "I won't be able to fill her mom's shoes, but I will try to be there for her." After that, as they walked down Front street, one of them would briefly comment about something in the window of a store or something else they observed, but mostly they were silent as they walked. It was a comfortable silence with neither one feeling compelled to break it. Davis could not remember feeling more relaxed in the past few months than he felt now.

When they returned to the front porch, Deidre told him good night He went one way, she the other. "Don't let Jay keep you up all night. Send him over soon,"

Laughing and talking, Amy and Jay were sitting on the sofa with a container of popcorn on the table in front of them when Deidre returned to the apartment. Soft music was coming from the CD player. Each giving the other undivided attention, they barely noticed her as she walked through. *As it should be with two young people in love,* she thought when she moved to her bedroom.

The young woman kicked off her shoes, picked up a book she had recently started laying down on her bed. Propping herself up with pillows Deidre found her marker at the place where she had left off the previous night and started reading. She read for a couple of minutes, but soon her thoughts began to get in the way of the words on the pages. "Davis is such a nice man." She was not sure if she had spoken the words or just thought the thought.

God, why can't you put someone like him in my life? What are the traits that make him so appealing? She wondered as she placed her book on the bed beside her. She decided that while he is attractive enough, he is not particular handsome. Rather than an outgoing personality he is rather quiet and laid back. He is very intelligent, but certainly not brilliant. He is ambitious, but he will never be wealthy. So why did she think so highly of him? She wasn't sure. Maybe it was because he seemed so real. What you see is what you get. Maybe it was because he so loved his late wife and his daughter. Perhaps it was because he knew how to treat people. He was in every sense a gentleman and that had always impressed her in a man. Perhaps the reason she liked him so much was because he was not a one dimensional person. Most of the men she had known in the past had one or two nice features, but the total package left something to be desired. While Davis certainly wasn't perfect, he was a more complete person than most of the men or even people she had known. Maybe that is what maturity is all about she decided.

Who knows what could have come of it if only he were ten or twelve years younger and wasn't my roommate's father, she told herself. Deidre had almost given up on dating, at least for awhile. She went out with Kevin Adams, a fellow teacher, three times recently, but she knew nothing could come of their relationship. He was nice enough, but a couple of years younger than she, his immaturity made him seem much younger than his twenty-six years. He had been much too aggressive on their third date. She had already decided that if he did call again, which she doubted, she would politely turn him down. *I'm going to have to put my future back in the Father's hands,* she decided. She had learned to trust the Lord early in life, but still got into trouble sometimes when she tried too hard to work things out on her own. Deidre again picked up her book as she heard the laughter of the young couple coming from the front room. *Oh Well, no one ever said life is easy. My time will come! I suppose somewhere out there the Lord has someone for me; I just wish he would send him my way while I can still recognize him when he arrives.*

Chapter 8

Deciding to alter his Monday routine to remain in town, Davis got up early, shaved, showered and dressed. Jay, who he had heard come in sometime after 1:00 a.m. was still sleeping. Davis left him a note on the kitchen table telling him to make himself at home. The note gave him permission to use whatever he could find in the kitchen to make himself breakfast. Davis then set out for the Little Rock Café. He had not joined the guys for breakfast in sometime.

Jay got up when he heard Mr. Morgan leave the house. He was sure his fiancé's father did not like him very much. The young man did not want to have to face him this morning, so he played possum until he knew he was gone. He went into the bathroom to take a shower moving back into the bedroom where he dressed. Jay wished Amy had not had to be in school today. It would have been nice to spend these morning and after-noon hours with her. He would have to find something to do on his own. Amy rode to school with Deidre leaving him her car. Perhaps he would drive to the mall in Rome. He had not been there before, but how hard would it be to find? First he would drive to one of the fast food places for breakfast. He didn't know where he would go from there, but it didn't really matter as long as he could get away from Mr. Morgan.

There was a barrage of good natured ribbing when Davis arrived at the Little Rock... "The prodigal has returned," Dean Nelson declared when he walked in.

"We thought the bomber must have gotten you after all," Red Edwards, owner of the Adairsville Hardware store, jested.

Brad Dewelt, the fire chief since he was a young man in his early thirties was not going to be outdone by the others. "Now that you are seeing that rich widow, we figured we were below your social level. We thought maybe you are ashamed to be seen with us."

"If this keeps up, it will probably be longer than two weeks before I join you guys again," Davis told them with a shy smile on his face.

"Don't let them get to you," the fourth member of the gang who was the best dressed of the group at the table, banker Al Jensen, encouraged him. "They are just jealous because exciting things are happening in your life while theirs continue to be boring.

"And I guess things down at the bank are exciting," Dean directed his remarks to Al.

"Probably as exciting as they are at your garage," his long time friend responded.

"I think I could do with a little less excitement in my life right now."

"That is not going to be the case as long as you are dating Tracie," Brad joked.

"You guys don't miss anything do you?"

"If it happens in Adairsville, we know about it." Dean spoke with a volume that made it possible for almost everyone in the little café to hear him. Davis thought of the phase that Julie often repeated for Amy's benefit when she was a child. When Amy got too loud she would quietly tell her, "Use your indoor voice".

"I have no reason to doubt that." Davis responded to Dean's statement without reminding him that he was indoors.

When Davis took the fifth and last chair at the large round table, the waitress approached it with pad and pencil. "May I take your orders?" she asked. "Or maybe you guys are going to just sit around and cluck like a bunch of old hens this morning."

"You've got these guys' number," Davis told Brenda the waitress.

"I've been trying to get her to give me her number for years," Red smiled at the feisty young lady.

"I doubt I'll ever be that hard up," she retorted.

"There goes your tip for today," Red laughed.

"I don't know how I will make it without that dime," she cracked.

The good natured conversation continued as each man gave his order to the young waitress who was never too busy to banter with the five gentlemen whose dignity seemed to cease to be a concern when they were together. After Brenda returned with their meals the conversation turned toward more serious matters. "Davis, have our local heroes made any progress toward solving Ed's murder?"

"Not much that I can see. Having a brother on the force, Dean can probably tell you more about that than I can."

"My brother doesn't tell me anything," Dean growled. "I don't even see him very often."

"Has he gone back to work yet," Al asked.

"I think he went back this morning."

"That's a good boy who is going to make us a fine chief someday," Brad predicted.

"You've got that right," someone said. Each man seemed to agree.

Red looked at Davis. "With everything that has happened to you recently, I bet you wish you were back in that Indiana church preaching."

"I am beginning to feel a little like Jonah." Davis made reference to the Old Testament Bible character thrown overboard by his companions and swallowed by a great fish when he tried to run away from his duty.

"You never told us why you left it," Dean spoke up. "From what I hear you were a big shot up there in Indiana, and everybody knows preachers only work one day a week. Man, you had it made!"

"Yeah," Davis snapped back. "I had it made. I got up many mornings about 5:30 in order to make it to the hospital before someone had surgery. I spoke several times a week and that required hours of preparation. You guys know me. I had a hard time talking to my wife if I didn't prepare for it. I did thirty funerals a year and about that many weddings. I was expected to make almost twenty nursing home visits every month and probably twice that many hospital visits. And in the midst of it all, I was always insecure about my job because I knew there were church members whose image of a pastor was far different than their impression of me. I never went on vacation confident I would have a job when I returned. That's when most preachers get fired you know, when they are away."

"Man! I'm sorry I asked," Dean shook his head. "You make it sounds like it wasn't a lot of fun."

Immediately ashamed of his negative outburst, Davis apologized, "I'm sorry guys, I didn't mean to give you such a drab picture of the ministry. I do consider it a special calling. The Lord did bless me with a good deal of satisfaction during those years. I believe we accomplished some good in the lives of a lot of people and that pleases me. It is true that serving a church can be a tough job, but I loved every thing about it." Taking a moment to think about the statement he just made, Davis back tracked a bit. "Maybe not 'every thing about it', but the experience was great. I would make the same decision if I were starting out today. I have no regrets. It's just that I don't think I can hack it anymore without Julie's help."

"You really miss her, don't you?" Red asked.

"I sure do. You guys can't imagine how hard it is to lose someone you love more than life itself. I get up each morning just sort of going though the motions. I don't believe five minutes ever go by without my thinking about her. I find myself needing her over and over, but she is never there. In the past year I have sometimes wondered, what's the point? It has been hard, but I think I am finally starting to learn to cope. But even that sometimes makes me feel as if I am betraying Julie."

Everyone at the table sit silently for a few moments not knowing how to respond. Finally it was Al who offered a feeble attempt to lighten the conversation. "It is probably a good thing you left the ministry, Davis. I can't see Tracie as a preacher's wife."

"You guys are bound and determined to make my life miserable, aren't you?

"You know you love every minute of it," Dean told him. "By the way, have you started the great American novel yet?"

"Not yet. Maybe I'll start it when Jay, my future son-in-law leaves."

"I enjoyed your column about your mom. It was great," Al praised the recently published column. "Miss Elaine was everything you declared her to be."

"She did the flowers for my wedding," Dean reminisced. "It must have been two years before we finished paying her, and then it probably wasn't half what another florist would have charged."

"Don't the parents of the bride pay for the wedding?" Red asked?

"Not Sherrie's parents. Even if they had been able to afford it, they would not have paid for Sherrie to marry me. They were disappointed their little girl didn't do better," Dean explained.

"I can understand that," Red wisecracked.

"Incidentally" Davis said. "If you don't mind me changing the subject...."

"I don't mind at all," Dean interrupted.

"Thanks," Davis said. "Now what was I going to ask? Oh, yeah. Do any of you guys know anything about this Mr. Brown who has been asking questions all over town?"

None of the men had any knowledge of him. "What kind of questions is he asking?" Red wanted to know.

"He is interested in our town history especially in the early 20th century," Davis explained.

"He must be hard up for hobbies," Brad remarked. "From what I hear I can't think of anything duller than Adairsville during that time."

"It got a whole lot more interesting in the eighties when we came of age," someone suggested. From there the conversation went to the exploits of the five men when they were much younger, some was fact and some obviously fiction.

"Well, I've got to get to work." Dean stood after remaining at the table as long as he dared. "I have a transmission to replace."

"Don't forget the tip," Al reminded the men as they began to disperse.

"That's just like a banker, always thinking about money," Dean accused as he walked toward the cash register with his wallet in hand.

Going by the post office to check his box for mail and purchase a roll of stamps, Davis returned home to find Jay gone. Amy and Deidre had long since left for school. He decided Amy must have left her car for Jay to use while she was at school. He was glad he would not have to spend the remainder of the morning entertaining his future son-in-law.

Even though Davis had only recently opened his shop, he had been in the book business for years. Being a persistent scout, in order to afford the books he wanted Davis had often searched for and found works dealers needed for their customers. He sometimes joked that his business was a hobby that got out of hand. Book people, like people in some other fields, have the tendency to bond through their mutual interest which is often an obsession. Charley had said that Mr. Brown's home base was Boston. He had a bibliophile friend in Boston. Wyman was a doctor, an M.D., but his love of books had led him first into collecting, and then into selling. He had the money to invest. His "hobby" turned out to be rather profitable. He sold Davis some good "Southern stock" at a great price before Davis opened his shop. Maybe I'll give him a call and see if he can get some information for me, Davis decided.

"Dr. North is extremely busy," Davis was told by the receptionist when he called Wyman's medical office. In a strictly business tone she told him, "I will take your number and have the Doctor return your call at a convenient time."

Ten minutes had barely passed when Davis' telephone rang. "Hello Davis, this is Wyman. What can I do for you?"

"I thought you were extremely busy. I expected it to be at least a month before you returned my call," Davis said sarcastically.

"I've always got time for you, buddy."

"You being a busy man, I'll get to the point. I need for you to see if you can dig up information on a Boston private investigator by the name of Brown. That is all I know about him."

"What kind of information do you need?"

"Anything you can get."

"You haven't given me much to work with, but I'll see what I can do. I'll get back to you."

"I would be eternally grateful."

"Just give me forty instead of the customary twenty percent dealer discount the next time you have something I need," he suggested.

"We'll talk about it when the time comes. By the way, I sold the signed Dickens the other day."

"How much you get for it?"

"Would you believe eight thousand?"

"Don't tell me that! I would have given you ten."

"You should have made me an offer. He who hesitates…you know."

"It's too late to do anything about that now. I'll get back to you if I find anything about this Brown. Take it easy pal." Davis heard the click on the other end of the line.

As usual, Davis enjoyed his Monday evening dinner with Amy and Deidre. The down side was Jay, but then even that wasn't too bad. With Amy occupied by Jay, he and Deidre had an opportunity to talk. She is an exceptional girl, he thought. But that's what she is, a girl; A very beautiful, wise, and gracious girl, but a girl nevertheless.

The ideal of a new vehicle had been lingering in Davis' mind since the embarrassment of driving Tracie to Barnsley Gardens in his old Ford. The mileage was approaching one hundred seventy-five thousand. It had been dependable, but he knew anything else he got out of the car which Julie had helped him pick out was a bonus. Selling the Dickens's book gave him a little extra cash that could be used as a down payment. He did not want to again start making car payments, but he knew it was inevitable.

Since he was a very young man Davis had desired to own a Jeep Wrangler. Early on he could not afford such a vehicle. In those days he drove the best deal he could get. Later when he was a pastor, it just was not practical. A Jeep Wrangler leading a funeral procession would have been a little strange. Now there was no reason why he should not get his Jeep. "There is a popular Jeep dealership in Jasper, about fifty-five miles east into the mountains", Davis told Jay on Tuesday evening. "Would you like to drive up there with me in the morning? I don't know if I am ready to buy, but I sure would like to take a look."

Jay agreed to go, so they left before eight o'clock Wednesday morning arriving at the dealership a little past nine. There were Jeep Wranglers everywhere they looked. A salesman wearing white shoes determined to make a sale latched unto them. They looked at more than twenty jeeps. There were green Jeeps, blue Jeeps, and Davis' favorite red Jeeps. Davis liked them all, but when he looked at the price stickers of even the less expensive of the vehicles, he announced to the salesman, "I want one, and eventually I will purchase one, but I think I need to wait a while longer. Davis and Jay left the lot with the salesman following them all the way back to his old Ford trying to make a deal. They laughed about the aggressive salesman almost all the way back to Adairsville. They passed a milestone that day. They spend time together without either of them being miserable. At lunch they both declared they would someday drive a Jeep Wrangler. Each man seemed to feel better about the other.

The next three days were pretty much routine, There was opportunity one afternoon for Davis to play eighteen holes of golf with his young preacher friend, John Redmond. Having never had a lot of time in the past to work on his game, Davis was no better than an average golfer. John; on the other hand, had been on his high school golf team. He continued to play once and sometimes twice a week. The result was that Davis was soundly beaten by seven strokes, but despite being taken to the cleaners he did enjoy time spent with the vibrant young preacher. There was even time to discuss some minor theological differences. Davis wished Amy had chosen someone like the personable redhead to marry. This outing that enabled him to get better acquainted with his preacher only elevated his opinion of his redheaded friend. The time on the links enabled Davis to get his mind off other matters. "Let's do this again," he suggested to John as he was pulling his clubs out of the trunk of John's car. Davis enjoyed the game, but had learned long ago the degree of enjoyment was very closely tied to the identity of the partner, or as in this case, his opponent for the day. When night came the tired golfer went to bed early sleeping relatively well for a change.

Chapter 9

A talkative middle aged lady brought in three boxes of books just before closing time on Thursday. Davis went home, but returned to his shop after dinner to go through his newly purchased items that had sat for years in storage after their former owner's death. He was unfamiliar with some of the titles and a few were not in very good condition, but he gave the daughter-in-law of the original owner, who brought them in, a good price because several leather bound volumes published in the middle 1800s were in the lot. The content was nothing special, but that doesn't really matter with nice leather bound copies. The reality is they are often purchased only for decorative purposes. Davis was anxious to get back to his place of business to dust and polish his newly acquired treasures. It was almost as if he could not bear to leave them in their present uncared for state any longer than necessary.

It was a rainy night. Davis got wet running the short distance from his car to the door. How often had Julie reminded him through the years to take an umbrella with him? But then there were many things he was prone to forget without Julie's prompting. Some of the lights were on. Davis could hear noise coming from upstairs where the drama group was putting the finishing touches on "Little Women" before their first performance the following evening. Davis had been looking forward to that all week, not so much because of the production. The stage version of Louisa May Alcott's story was something he could take or leave, but his excitement stemmed from the anticipation of again being with Tracie for the evening.

Sitting at his computer Davis checked the value of several of the purchases he made earlier. He was disappointed with what he learned about several of them, but was pleased to find that a couple of the Jesse Stuart titles, both first editions signed would bring a good return on his investment. He wrote the prices lightly with pencil on the first white page of each volume. He then went to work on the leather bound copies, applying neutral colored shoe polish. He used a rag to rub the covers to a nice shine. He was pleased with the results. They were worth every cent he paid for them. He reasoned that they would not remain on his shelves very long. Several of the actors, having finished their rehearsal, spoke to him as they left. "I took care of the lights upstairs," Ryan Blackwood, the director, told him on his way out. "Will you lock the front door when you leave?"

"I'll take care of it," he assured the short, balding drama teacher from one of the area colleges. "Be careful, it's storming pretty badly out there."

After everyone had gone, Davis began to get that eerie, spooky feeling he always got at night when he was in the old building alone.

As the lightening flashed and the thunder cracked, for obvious reasons his mind turned to "The Phantom of the Opera" which he and Julie had enjoyed on a trip to New York several years back. "Who knows what's lurking in the shadows in this old theater?" He spoke out loud with the deepest and spookiest voice he could muster and then laughed to himself. Deciding he needed some company, he switched on his radio turning the dial to where he knew the Braves were broadcast. *If they are playing in Atlanta, they were, no doubt, rained out, but I think they are playing in Philadelphia,* he told himself.

He was right, "Braves 2 – Phillies 2," he heard Don Sutton, one of the broadcasters, announce after a couple of minutes. After finishing his polishing, he went to the storage closet to retrieve some cleaner which he used to remove price stickers from dust jackets. While in the small room he did some rearranging wondering how such areas can get so disorganized and cluttered almost overnight. Walking with his head down Davis returned to his work table. When he looked up he came to a quick halt and took a step backwards. His heart must have missed a beat or two. In front of him, in the dim light, was the shape of a man. The figure was about six feet tall, slightly heavy, and dressed in black pants and a short sleeve white shirt. He had something in his right hand. It took Davis only a moment to realize that the object he held was an umbrella which brought an immediate sigh of relief from Davis' throat.

"I saw your light. The door was unlocked, so I just came on in," Mr. Brown explained. "I hope I didn't startle you."

"No, not at all." Davis fibbed still feeling weak from the shock he had received at the sudden appearance of the mysterious man from Boston. "You really should not be in here. We are closed you know."

"I understand that," he said. "I'm not here to purchase anything. I'll only take a moment of your time. I saw your column about your mother. It was well written. You have a way with words." Mr. Brown complimented him.

"Thank you," Davis responded. "I don't know how good I am, but I do get a lot of enjoyment from writing."

"'Miss Elaine' must really have been something." His plastic grin along with the tone of his voice made Davis a little uneasy.

Davis was at a loss for words. "Indeed she was."

"I gather from your column that she was not born around here."

"She came here from near Philadelphia when she was in her early teens." Davis, getting more irritated with each moment, told his visitor. "What is this all about anyway?"

Mr. Brown ignored the question asking still another of his own. "When would that have been? When did she arrive in Adairsville?"

"It would have been around 1940, maybe a little after that." His voice now reflected his irritation. "Sir, I'm not going to answer any more of your questions until you tell me why you are so curious."

"I can't say now, but I can assure you that it is to your advantage to cooperate with me."

"What do you mean?"

"That is all I can reveal at the present time," he declared.

"Then I think it best that you be on your way, Mr. Brown," Davis was more assertive now having regained his composure after the initial shock had subsided

"Good night, Mr. Morgan. I'll be in touch." His tone was polite as he was already slowly walking toward the door with a slight limp Davis had not noticed before. The entire building lit up from the lightening, and there was a loud crack of thunder. I think it's time I locked the doors and went home, Davis told himself. Pressing the power button on the radio he moved toward the door where he punched his code into the alarm system, cut off the lights and secured the building.

On Friday morning, Davis took Jay who had to be back in Orlando for a meeting late that afternoon, to the airport. *He is growing on me,* Davis decided as his future son-in-law whom he had taken to breakfast a couple of times and lunch once earlier in the week, sat silently moping in the passenger seat. "You already miss her, don't you?" Davis asked in reference to Amy.

"You bet I do. I love her so much. It's hard to be separated."

"Well, it will not be for long. Did the two of you decide on a date for the wedding?"

"It's going to be the last Saturday in August if the church is not being used for something else that day. Amy will call John today to check on the availability."

"Is your company still willing to transfer you to Atlanta in September?" Davis asked with more than passing interest.

"As far as I know, that's still the plan. If they balk, I shouldn't have a problem finding as good or even better position with a company in the Atlanta area. I don't want Amy to have to relocate. She is very happy with her job as well as the community. I refuse to spoil her happiness."

Davis breathed a sigh of relief. "I think you will enjoy living in this area. I do, but I have to admit I am biased since I grew up here. It is a pretty long commute to Atlanta, but a lot of people who live in Adairsville make it every day and live through it."

"I can be satisfied anywhere as long as Amy is with me," Jay told his future father-in-law.

"That is what I want to hear. I think I'm going to enjoy having you in the family, Jay." Davis found it hard to believe those words were coming from his mouth, and even harder to believe they were coming from his heart. They hit the morning rush hour traffic toward the end of its peak being slowed slightly at times before they reached the airport, but not really delayed. They arrived in plenty of time for Jay to catch his flight. Davis dropped him off at the curb in front of the north terminal feeling a little sad at the young man's departure. He drove the seventy miles back to Adairsville listening to his show tunes CD dreaming about dinner, "Little Women," and a beautiful blond with dimples.

Upon his return, Davis decided he would give Wyman North a call to see if he had learned anything about Mr. Brown. This time he got through to Wyman on the first try. "I can't believe I got past that receptionist of yours. I don't remember that ever happening before," he told his friend.

"She is a good one. I have to say that because she is standing next to me right now," he joked.

"I was wondering if you have learned anything about Mr. Brown." Davis didn't waste any time in getting to the reason for his call.

"I've been meaning to give you a ring. Actually my receptionist did most of the research. She found that Brown has a good reputation around the city. He seems to be a decent human being, unlike many of those in Boston calling themselves Private Investigators. He does most of his work for five or six legal firms here in the greater Boston area."

"I don't suppose you came across any information about why he is in Georgia did you?"

"No, I doubt I can help you there."

"Well, I appreciate what you have told me."

"I hope it helps."

"It does. Thanks again and be sure to tell your receptionist I appreciate what she did for me. I'll talk with you soon."

Davis' curiosity was heightened about the investigator. Why his interest in Adairsville history? What kind of business did he have with Tracie? Why all the questions about "Miss Elaine?" Does any of it tie into Ed's murder and the bombing of his house? Pondering those questions, Davis made himself a sandwich going to the refrigerator for a Diet Coke after which he went to the shop until closing time at five o'clock.

Returning to his apartment he showered, shaved for the second time that day, and put on his best blue suit with his favorite tie. He was ready for his date with the lovely Tracie Ennis. Amy had suggested he drive her car. He eagerly accepted the offer. Less than a year old, it would make a better impression than his ancient Ford. Knocking on Amy's apartment door, Davis waited. "Come on in, called his daughter. You look like you are ready for a heavy date," she kidded her dad. "Come in here Deidre. Take a look at the most handsome man in North Georgia."

Deidre came into the living room from her bedroom. "I concur," she smiled. "I can't imagine there being a more distinguished looking gentleman anywhere in these parts." A little disappointed, Davis frowned. "Distinguished" wasn't the look he was going for since it reminded him of his age. He and Amy exchanged keys. Davis put the keys in his pocket aware as he always was when he drove Amy's car of the small pepper spray canister on the key chain. He was glad she carried it for safety reasons, but he was afraid the lever would get pushed out of the safety position while in his pocket causing him to end up getting sprayed with the irritating spray.

Amy's sporty vehicle was fun to drive. It would provide a much more appropriate ride for Tracie than his worn out old car. About half way up the mountain Davis spotted a vehicle stopped in the middle of the narrow road with the hood raised. He slowed down, and then stopped, not being able to get around it. Getting out he walked around to the front of the medium sized car. Davis approached a man probably in his middle fifties. The first thing he noticed about the stranger was his small mustache and obscure chin; features which caused him to look a little like a rat. In the split second before approaching him, Davis laughed to himself remembering a mystery story one of his elementary teachers read to the class in which the villain was called the "rat faced man." The stranded motorist looked exactly as he had imagined that villain looking. That thought made him a little ashamed of himself.

"What's your trouble?" Davis asked.

"You are, Morgan?" The "rat faced man" snarled as he turned toward Davis pulling a gun from his belt. A partner, younger and heavier than the "rat faced man" came up behind Davis, also armed.

Chapter 10

The man behind him poked the weapon into Davis' ribs, grabbed his arm turning him around while pushing him back in the direction from which he came. He forced Davis back into Amy's car on the driver's seat. The "rat faced man" got into the passenger side still holding the gun. "You follow him." He pointed to the big man who lowered the hood of the other vehicle and got under the steering wheel. Davis, with an accelerating heart rate, started the engine without saying a word.

"We should have taken care of you that night at Hagan's house," said the "rat faced man" with a voice that could only be described as gravelly. "We wouldn't be having all this trouble now." He gruffly spit out his words as if he were thoroughly disgusted. With his captor beside him urging him to do so, Davis followed closely the driver ahead of him. He recognized Tracie's house off to the right as they drove past. "I understand we almost got you by accident with the bomb," his captor laughed. "That would have been ironic."

"What is this about? What do you guys want with me?" Davis demanded.

"You are an inconvenience for a friend of ours," the rat faced" man, told him. "Better turn your lights on. You wouldn't want to have an accident ending up getting hurt would you?"

His attempt at sarcasm didn't impress Davis. "How am I an inconvenience and to whom?" Davis asked turning on his headlights.

"There is no reason for you to ever know. It is best you keep your mouth shut and do what you are told." Driving five or six miles farther, Davis made two right turns. He recognized the area as being near one of his favorite boyhood camp sites. He and several of his rowdy friends had pitched a tent near here more than a few times. A couple of times they had climbed into the belfry of a small church nearby to catch pigeons. The birds would roost in the belfry of the little country church. The light of a strong flashlight turned directly on them would freeze them so they could be captured with relative ease. Later when the boys grew tired of taking care of them, the birds would be released.

It had been more than twenty-five years since Davis had been along this isolated section of the county. The driver in front of him pulled off the main road to the right into a small overgrown drive probably used for farm purposes in the past. Davis' heart was pumping hard in his chest. *This is it, he thought. This is where it all comes to an end. "Lord, if I ever needed your help, I need it now."* He prayed silently. He felt a calmness wash over him as God's Word flowed through his brain. *"What gain is there in my destruction, in my going down into the pit? Will the dust praise you? Will it proclaim your faithfulness?"* (Psalm 30:9)

Following the lead car into the rough drive Davis stepped on the brake pedal; He turned off the engine, and took the keys in his right hand. The "rat faced man" marched him over to the other car where he reached through the open door to get something that Davis quickly identified as a roll of duct tape. "You stay here he told the other man. I'll take care of him. Let's go." He motioned with his weapon for Davis to go into the pines to the left. "Keep walking." Maybe a hundred and fifty feet into the woods he declared, "That's far enough!"

"What are you going to do?" Davis knew full well what his plans were.

"Get on your knees and put your hands behind you!"

Up to this point Davis had kept the car keys in his right hand. He now dropped them. His mind gave him a vivid picture of Ed Hagan the night he found him in the bathroom. No doubt this obviously vicious killer made him kneel in his bathroom, taped his hands behind him, put the gun to the back of his head and pulled the trigger. The "rat faced man" now had Davis' arms behind him starting to wrap tape around his wrist. Until this moment Davis had been too stunned to be anything but passive. It was now crystal clear to him that he would be dead in the next few moments if he did not act. Being close to the ground, on his knees, his eyes focused on the keys he had dropped now lying two feet to his left. He dropped to the ground in a position where it was possible for him to get his hands on the keys. He was lying on his side with his face away from his assailant.

The angry villain grabbed the collar of Davis' jacket pulling in an effort to get him back on his knees. Davis, with his thumb, turned the lever on the tube of pepper spray Amy carried on her key chain, releasing it from the safety position he mashed hard. He desperately moved his arms trying to get his taped hands near the man's face where the spray would do its job. His would be assassin was yelling and cursing. Davis was on his feet by this time knowing the other killer would be there quickly. He ran into the woods as fast as he could with hands bound behind him. "Morgan," he heard the "rat faced man" shouting. "You're a dead man."

Davis continued to blindly run through the trees and bushes. The darkness made it difficult, but he was glad for the overcast night knowing it made it hard for the two murderers to see him. The noise he was making as he ran drowned out any sound behind him, but he knew they were coming. He stumbled over something, perhaps a fallen log, but quickly got to his feet. He was thankful he was still in full dress when he felt his jacket being snagged by the vines and briars. *Better his jacket than his flesh.*

He could see an open field in front of him. Breathing hard, he ran toward that open space with all the strength he had. He did not realize that the field was a pasture surrounded by a barbed wire fence until he ran full speed into the wire bouncing backward to the ground. He had to keep going. Staying on the ground for only a moment, he simply rolled under the bottom strand of wire, got to his feet and began to run again. There were several cows ahead. Running toward the unsuspecting live stock caused them to scatter. Perhaps his pursuers could be confused by ten or twelve cows lumbering in different directions. Out in the open he knew he might be a clear target. He half expected to feel a bullet going through his back at any moment.

Seeing the little church up ahead off to his right, Davis suddenly knew where he was. Perhaps houses had been built near by since he had been there as a boy, but he saw no lights. He remembered that someone lived close enough to hear the church bell because one of his friends had accidentally grabbed the rope when they were in the belfry on one of their pigeon hunt adventures. That had brought the police in a matter of minutes as well as an escort home which had not pleased his mom.

This time when Davis came to a barbed wire fence he stopped. He rolled under it continuing to lie on the ground for a moment to rest. Knowing he needed to get moving in order to stay ahead of his pursuers, he got to his feet running toward the little white frame church building. The door was never locked when he and his friends had been there years ago, but it was now. He kicked the door hard with the bottom of his right foot. It gave slightly, but stayed intact. He kicked a second and then a third time before it finally broke open. Such abuse of a house of worship bothered him, even with his life hanging by a thread.

In the darkness, Davis ran straight toward the space where one could climb into the belfry. He hoped the rope was still there. He backed into the wall feeling for the rope with his taped hands. He felt it hit his shoulder. Bending forward, he raised his hands so high it was painful, but got hold of the rope pulling for fifteen to twenty seconds. The ring of the bell was strong. Surely someone would hear it and call the police.

He also knew his two pursuers would come straight to the little church when they heard the bell. They could come through the door at any moment. He had to find a place where he could successfully hide for a few minutes until help got there, assuming it would. He headed toward the front platform. Hoping they hadn't remodeled, he lowered himself to the floor of the platform stretching out on his side. He lifted the edge of the rug feeling what he was hoping for. The baptistery was still under the platform accessible by lifting what looked like a large trap door. He remembered it because it was identical to the set up in his home church before they remodeled. The two edifices were probably built by the same contractor.

With his hands taped behind him, would he be able to raise the trap door high enough to get into the baptistery? *Surely they still drained the tank each time after use.* He could drown in there with his hands bound behind him if it contained water. Davis was able to pull the trap door high enough to get his left foot under it, then pushing the heavy door up with his foot he was able to squeeze under. As he fell, he knew immediately there was no water in the tank, but he almost wished there had been when he hit the bottom face down. The jolt left him unable to breathe for a few moments. The trap door had fallen back in place behind him. It would hide him for a little while, but how long would it take for the killers to figure it out. No doubt the rug was out of place. They could have been close enough to hear the noise of the trap door falling back into place or him hitting the bottom of the tank. He knew he would not be safe there for long. He lay silently still for three or four minutes before be began to hear voices. "We know you are in here Morgan. You're a dead man..." The noise told Davis the men were trashing the little church. He regretted that, but he preferred it to being dead.

How long would it take for the police to get there? Maybe no one heard the bell. Maybe they heard but did not call anyone. Perhaps the neighbors would come to investigate themselves only to be killed by the two murderers. His spirits were sinking lower and lower. Why did he get into the tank or even come into the building in the first place? He was trapped. The "rat faced man" was right, he was a dead man, but then there was silence. At least ten minutes passed without any noise whatsoever. Maybe they were gone or perhaps they were trying to make him think they had left the building.

Continuing to lay still Davis was almost afraid to breathe. Did he dare investigate? Common sense told him no. He lay there a few more minutes; however, eventually feeling as if he had to do something he began to get to his feet. The tank was probably less than four feet deep, so he was able to raise the trap door by standing to his feet and slowly straightening up. The heavy door falling backwards on its hinges made a loud noise when it hit the floor. He quickly climbed out of his hiding place using the steps in place for those coming and going into the pool when the ordinance of baptism was practiced. Then his worst fear became a reality. His two pursuers stepped into view in the back of the little sanctuary. "I thought you would come out if we stayed quiet for a little while," "the rat faced man" said in a tone that made it evident he was extremely peeved with Davis.

Facing his two assailants, Davis caught a glimpse of light coming through the windows behind them. It was headlights! The men became aware of the lights about the same time as he, both glancing backwards. Davis took advantage of the split second he had, turning and running full speed toward the large window to his left. He heard a shot ring out just before he went airborne, crashing through the window with glass going in every direction. Not really knowing if the villain's bullet had entered any part of his body, Davis assumed he was not wounded when he was able to get to his feet quickly to immediately put as much distance as possible between him and the church. By this time the approaching car stopped. Two people in uniform were running in his direction. He stopped running when he realized it was the chief along with Charley. "I'll hug both of you if you cut my hands loose," Davis said in a tone that must have expressed some of the relief he felt.

"That you, Davis?" Charley cried out, recognizing his friend's voice. "What are you into now?"

"Two men tried to kill me," he responded suddenly realizing that the "rat faced man" and his partner had probably run in the opposite direction when the two cops came to his rescue. "If we hurry we can get to where they are parked before they get away," he shouted.

Charley already had his pocket knife out cutting the tape from Davis' hands. They ran to the patrol car. The two officers got in the front seat with the chief driving. Davis got into the back seat. "You tell me where to go," the chief barked.

It was not until then that Davis realized he was not sure how to get back to the spot where he had been bound, the spot where the two villains would surely be headed to retrieve their ride. In the back of the patrol car feeling the adrenalin draining from him, Davis silently thanked God for his deliverance. *"I will exalt you, O Lord, for you lifted me up out of the depths and did not let my enemies gloat over me."* (Psalm 30:1) Delayed by a couple of wrong turns, they found Amy's car where it had been left, but the other vehicle was gone.

Chapter 11

D avis was driven to the emergency room of the hospital in Rome where he first called Amy attempting to assure her he was okay. "Nothing but a few stitches," he told his concerned daughter who had to be convinced it was true.

He then called Tracie explaining why he had not kept their date while announcing she did not need to worry about him. "Everything is fine", he told her. Davis appreciated that there were people who had genuine concern for his welfare. Charley drove him back to Adairsville after the doctor on duty treated and stitched his cuts. Another officer took Amy's car to the police station. The policeman told Davis that after a fifteen minute search they found the keys where he had dropped them near where he had pepper sprayed his assailant.

"The chief has decided to keep an officer in front of your house at night and your shop during the day," Charley told him.

"You won't hear me object."

"We've got something to go on now that we have the descriptions you gave us. Maybe we can catch these killers and put an end to this madness soon."

"I sure hope so. I don't know how much more this old out of shape body can take, and I am expecting my insurance company to cancel me any day," Davis laughed.

When they arrived at Davis' front door, Charley reminded him of the new security measures. "You get a good night's sleep. I'll be out here all night."

Davis spent a couple of hours on Saturday morning making arrangements for repairs at the Crown Creek church that was damaged by him and his pursuers the previous night. Finding workers on Saturday was not easy. It would cost him more than he could afford, but he wanted as many of the repairs as possible made before the worshippers arrived on Sunday morning. One of the other officers had already relieved Charley when Davis went outside late in the morning. "I know this must be a pain for you guys. Your department isn't large enough to play nursemaid to me twenty-four hours a day."

I don't want to frighten you, Mr. Morgan," the officer told him, "But you can identify those killers. They are going to do one of two things. They will run as far away from here as they can, or they will come after you again. If they come after you, we want to be here."

"I want you to be there too," Davis smiled. "I'm going to be cautious, but I'll not be a prisoner in my own house." He had once heard someone in a movie say that. He immediately recognized how silly it sounded. "I'm going to the post office and then to the shop in a few minutes."

"I'll be right behind you," the officer assured him.

Davis was pleased to find checks from two different book dealers in his post office box. Some of the fruit from last week's effort. It was good to know all the time spent putting information on one of the on line book sites was not wasted. Maybe someday his business in the shop would be so good that he would not have to do that, but for now the internet was an important part of his business strategy. After getting to the shop, Davis called Tracie. "You want to try again tonight?" he asked after his initial greeting.

"What is it you want to try again tonight?" Tracie inquired laughing.

"I was thinking we might again attempt to see "Little Women," he suggested. "Janie says there are still tables available. Of course, I won't be able to wear what use to be my best suit, and I won't look my best with bandages and stitches all over my head and face, but I surely would like to spend some time with you."

"I'm game if you are up to it," she responded. "I think it would be more convenient for you and the police department if I met you there at seven o'clock."

"That sounds great to me. I can hardly wait to see you."

It was a busy Saturday at the Corra Harris Bookshop. He made three sales to a Joel Chandler Harris collector. He hated to let go of some books. Harris' interesting work on Georgia history and a very nice older copy of *The Tales of Uncle Remus* were two such items, but both brought him a nice profit as well as the third sale in the trio. Most of the other books he sold were inexpensive, less than ten dollars each, but he sold enough of them that the amount added up nicely.

Just before five o'clock closing time he received a telephone call. "Davis, this is Mr. Brown," the voice said. "I heard what happened to you last night. I think it's time we talked. I believe I can help you make sense of it all. Could I come by your place tonight? You can ask a policeman to be there if you like. I think they would also be interested in what I have to say."

Davis not wanting to break his date with Tracie on consecutive evenings told him, "I'll be tied up until about ten thirty, but I would like to meet with you then. I need to talk with you if you have information that will help me understand what this is all about."

"I'll be at your house at ten thirty."

"I sure would like to have you there," Davis suggested to Charley when he called the police station telling Charley about his plan to meet with Mr. Brown.

"I wouldn't miss it for the world," he told Davis. "It will work out well since I am scheduled to be your body guard tonight anyway."

"I guess I'll see you a little later then," Davis said hanging up.

Calling Tracie, Davis told her about his conversation with Mr. Brown hoping she would understand why he would need to keep their evening short.

"No problem," she assured him. "I understand."

Davis went home taking a good hour to get ready for his date. He went over to Amy and Deidre's apartment to let them know he would return before ten thirty. He also told them Mr. Brown would be showing up about that time. He did not want them to panic if they happened to spot the stranger in their yard. "Will Charley be joining you and Tracie for dinner and the production?" Amy facetiously inquired. Having a policeman looking over your shoulder could cramp your style."

"He'll be in the building, but I don't think it will matter since I don't really have a style to cramp."

"You sell yourself short," Amy told him. "You are a very handsome man, and I've heard other ladies talk about your charm. Right, Deidre?"

"That's right," Deidre responded blushing.

Sherman Brown had the radio in his rental car tuned to the public radio station out of Atlanta he discovered earlier. The classical music coming through the speakers was a pleasant diversion for the Boston detective. He hated being away from home, but that was the nature of the beast. He estimated that seventy percent of his assignments took him outside of the city in which he lived. *That's okay,* he decided. *Less than two years and I can pack it all up.* He was looking forward to retirement. More time with his grandchildren would be a welcome change. Jane, his wife of almost forty years, had been patient. They would be able to do some traveling together once he retired. Already they were starting to plan an extended trip west. He had always wanted to see the Grand Canyon and she wanted to go to California. Surely there would be enough interesting detours between the two sites to keep them busy for days. *I've got to get to a store to find her a birthday gift,* Brown reminded himself as his mind turned to his wife. Wednesday would be her birthday. It looked like he would make it home for the festivities. He smiled when he considered how good it would be to have all the family, including the five grandchildren, together for dinner and a bit of a party at his home on Wednesday evening.

I wish Morgan could have met with me earlier. For once it would have been nice to have gotten into bed before midnight. Then recalling how uncomfortable he found the bed in his motel room, he decided the late hour was no big deal. His thoughts turned to Davis Morgan. *He has no idea of the extent of the danger he and his daughter are facing,* he told himself. Brown knew he probably should have explained what he had uncovered to the bookseller earlier, but he needed to be sure. Now that there was no doubt about the facts he would let Morgan and the police in on it.

The driver behind Brown was making him a little uneasy. The car continued to stay behind him even after he made three turns. Now the driver was getting a little close to his back bumper. He wished he had brought his gun, but when he left Boston he thought there was no way he would need it… and getting permission to travel with a gun on a commercial airline in today's world was a real hassle. He would sure feel safer with the gun knowing what he now knew. Up ahead Brown saw a car stalled. Someone is having mechanical problems he surmised when he observed the hood raised with a man under it. *I'll stop and see if he needs some help. That will give me the opportunity to check out the intentions of the vehicle behind me.* He pulled in behind the stalled car. When he opened the door to climb out, a pain shot through the upper thigh of his left leg, a little reminder of his time in Vietnam. "Can I help you?" He asked the stranded motorist.

"There is no reason for you to waste your gas" Charley suggested to Davis. They rode together in the patrol car the short distance to the 1902 Stock Exchange. It was still twenty minutes before anyone would be allowed upstairs to the theater, but already a number of people who had assembled for dinner and the evening's entertainment were milling about looking at the merchandise in the various shops. He was pleased that several people were browsing in the Corra Harris Bookshop. "That's what I like about theater nights," he told Charley. "The shops are kept open for an hour before dinner and for a few minutes after the production. It creates the potential for more sales." But Charley, already giving his attention to Janie, did not acknowledge his statement.

It was five minutes till seven when Tracie arrived. She looked more beautiful than Davis could ever remember her being before, and she had always been something special. He immediately became self conscience of his own appearance which was less than appealing with stitches and bandages on his face and head from his encounter with "the rat faced' man and his partner, but Tracie quickly made him forget his ugly wounds. Davis decided Tracie could enable a man to forget just about anything.

The evening was delightful. The catered buffet which featured both roast beef and chicken was perfect. He and Tracie reminisced about their high school years. They laughed a lot. For a time Davis completely forgot about the "rat faced" man, Mr. Brown, and everything that had happened the last three weeks. The production of "Little Women" was well done making Davis proud of several of the actors he knew personally. He was very much aware of Tracie's soft hand covering the top of his own throughout most of the program. They continued to sit at the table for a few minutes as the crowd dispersed. "Davis, you are making quite an impression on this lonely little Southern girl," Tracie told him looking directly into his eyes.

"I hope so," he responded. "I do want to spend a lot of time with you. I think I have been the happiest these past few weeks when you have been around." By now all the guests had left the theater leaving only the two of them and three ladies, each rolling carts onto which they were stacking glasses and plates from the vacated tables. Tracie, always the uninhibited one, learned toward Davis, her soft lips touching his. She pulled away a moment later at the sound of glasses jingling nearby. Davis wanted to tell the lady collecting the glasses to go do something else, but he didn't.

They got up, walked down the winding staircase finding Charley at the checkout counter still talking to Janie. "Have you been pestering Janie all evening?" Davis asked.

"I haven't been pestering her. I have been wooing her!"

"He is a real Romeo," the good natured clerk said. "If we ever do *Romeo and Juliet* here, he's got the Romeo part for sure."

Tracie and Davis walked together to the door. They said good night with a quick kiss, not as tender, and not as memorable as the one five minutes earlier; nevertheless, delightful.

"You ready to go?" Davis asked Charley. "It's almost ten thirty."

"I'll try to tear myself away from this lovely lady," Charley said directing his charming smile to Janie.

"'Farewell, farewell, parting is such sweet sorrow,'"

Charley took a seat in his living room while Davis prepared his coffee maker to brew an Irish Cream blend of gourmet coffee. Davis didn't need the caffeine, but he knew Charley as his body guard might need it in order to stay awake. It was after 10:30 when Davis poured cups for himself and Charley, but still no Mr. Brown. Eleven o'clock, eleven thirty and two cups of coffee apiece, he still had not arrived.

"I don't think he is coming," Charley surmised.

"I should have had him come on over when he called. I wish he had given me a number. I don't even know where he is staying."

"Check your caller ID on your cell," suggested Charley.

"He called me on my land line. I don't have caller ID on that."

"Well, I'll be outside if he does get here. You go ahead and get some sleep. I know you got very little last night," Charley got up to leave. "Sleep well," he said walking toward the front door. "I hope you dream about that beautiful blond, but then I suspect that is a foregone conclusion."

"You try to stay awake out there," Davis chided as he handed his friend a thermos containing what was left of the coffee. "A very important person's life is in your hands."

A decent night of sleep would be needed since Davis had given in to Ralph Hayes' rather insistent invitation to be guest speaker at the Crown Creek church the following morning. When Davis called the deacon about the needed repairs to the building as a result of his recent episode with "the rat faced" man, Ralph, knowing of Davis' past experience in the ministry, insisted that he fill the pulpit since they were without a pastor and their interim preacher had called in sick. Davis, at first, resisted the invitation, but with much reluctance finally gave in when Mr. Hayes declared that speaking that one Sunday was part of his penitence for damaging their church building. Davis' guilt was sufficient to motivate him to do something he really dreaded. Amy had spent a couple of hours earlier in the day calling most of his friends including Charley, Tracie and the gang from the Little Rock inviting them to the service to hear her dad speak.

To say Davis was nervous about the task ahead was an under statement. At this point in his life he felt unqualified for such a mission. That thought along with concerns about the message he planned to present kept him awake much of the night.

Chapter 12

Only four cars were in the graveled parking lot of the Crown Creek Church on Sunday morning when Davis, Amy and Deidre arrived for Bible study a few minutes till ten. The elderly Ralph Hayes met and greeted them when they walked through the front door. Ralph was one of those characters you didn't forget once you got to know him. His friend-liness stood out in any crowd. Davis had no idea of the man's age. It seemed to him that the bald slender gentleman was an old man more than thirty years ago when he first knew him. Ralph drove an old blue Chevy pick-up truck probably ten years old. When one got behind a long line of slow moving traffic anywhere in town Ralph could usually be found in the first vehicle of the caravan. He had outlived two wives marrying for the third time just a few months earlier. "This is my darling wife; Eleanor", Ralph spoke as he proudly presented a silver headed lady about a foot shorter than him and probably several years younger. She smiled extending her hand first to Davis and then to each of the young ladies.

As they walked though the small worship center which Ralph referred to as their sanctuary, Davis noticed that things had been put back in order nicely. He would have to compliment the crew of workers he had sent to the church the previous day. The only evidence he could see of his earlier ordeal with the two thugs at that location was the four foot by eight foot sheet of plywood covering the window which he had crashed through. "We could not match the glass. We had to order it." Ralph explained when he saw Davis looking in that direction.

Other people were starting to arrive. The three visitors were escorted to a classroom where adults of all ages assembled for Bible class. They were made to feel welcome by the twelve to fifteen people who eventually gathered there, all a great deal older than Davis and decades older than the girls. The lesson was from a portion of Jesus' Sermon on the Mount in Matthew six. Davis found the presentation enjoyable even though Bother Frank's lecture was anything but smooth. He obviously wasn't up on the latest methods. There was no power-point, overhead or technology of any type, but there was no doubt that the long-time teacher loved God's Word and had done some serious preparation. His no frills verse by verse explanation of the passage was superb.

When they returned to the "sanctuary" Davis observed that several of his friends had responded to Amy's invitation to hear him speak. He felt good about that, but for some reason also found it a little disconcerting. When he greeted Dean and his wife Sherrie during the break between Bible Study and worship, his friend with a teasing smile pointed to the window covered with plywood asking, "Your handy work?

Al, Red, and Brad were also present. Even Brenda, the waitress from the Little Rock was there with her two children along with Cindy who recently became Davis' barber. He later learned that Cindy and her family were members of the little church. With the entire Little Rock crowd present Davis chuckled to himself, wondering if he could expect to be heckled. Davis was disappointed that Charley was not in attendance, but his young friend could be excused since he had been on duty all night. The absence of Tracie constituted Davis' biggest let down. He and Tracie had not talked about spiritual matters. He was hoping her presence for today's service would open the door for such conversation. He was surprised to see the little building which probably seated only about a hundred and twenty people filled to capacity with the ushers sitting up folding chairs from the classrooms in the back.

"This is our best attendance since Easter," Ralph whispered to him. Sitting through several old hymns and a series of prayers did not calm Davis' nerves. While ministering to the church in Indiana Davis usually spoke to nearly four hundred people on Sunday mornings. He had twice made presentations at conventions with several thousand in attendance, but he had never been more uptight than right now as he waited to speak to this small group of worshippers that included friends and acquaintances he had known most of his life.

His hands were cold and clammy even though the temperature in the little sanctuary was rather warm. He took time to silently ask for God's help as Ralph's gracious introduction made him wonder who this super preacher was. *Lord, you know how inadequate I feel today. If ever I needed your help, I need it now. Help me be a blessing…*

Standing silently behind the pulpit for a few moments Davis surveyed his audience before speaking in his natural conversational tone. He attributed the first few words he spoke to a preacher he greatly admired, the late Peter Marshall. "We are told it is appointed unto men once to die. Yet it seems to me that we often approach life as if we think we will live forever. Casual observation should be enough to convince us that everything that has a beginning also has an ending. The day begins with sunshine, but after a time the shadows gather and the day is closed out, that particular day never to appear again. History tells us that nations and civilizations rise; flourish for a time and then decay sets in and finally destruction. All we have to do is look around us to see that all of nature is in the process of dying. Someone once suggested, 'we start to die the day we are born', but that is not bad news, at least not for the one in Christ. The Gospel is good news and part of that good news is what happens to the Christian after this life is over. In Christ there is going to be a great reunion, a homecoming like no other. We will move to a special place that the Bible calls *Heaven*."

It was obvious to the little congregation that Davis was starting to feel more confident now that he was into his message. Eventually he turned his Bible to Revelation reading John's vision of the "New Jerusalem" recorded in chapter twenty-one verses one through eight suggesting the passage reveals several reasons we can expect our final destination to be special.

"Heaven will be special because of the fellowship we will enjoy there. Who can we expect to find there when we arrive? Consider verse three of out text. 'And I heard a loud voice from the throne saying, 'now the dwelling of God is with men and he will live with them'."

"We will live with God; experiencing a never ending fellowship with the one we love most–the one who loves us most. But who else can we expect to be there?" Davis asked his attentive audience. "Verse seven says, 'He who overcomes will inherit all this and I will be his God and he will be my son'." Thinking especially of Julie and his own mother Davis declared, "All of God's children of all ages will be present when we arrive – Those that we have loved that have gone before us. Think about it! Together with God for all eternity will be the redeemed of all the ages."

The bookseller, still a preacher at heart, went on to speak of the benefits of the Christian's final home. "He will wipe away every tear from their eyes. There will be no more death or mourning or crying. We will never again have to gather in a church or funeral home somewhere to say goodbye to a loved one. We are also told there will be no pain in Heaven." Davis remembered the pain that Julie had so graciously handled through out the last days of her life and silently thanked the Lord she no longer had to endure such torture.

Davis pointed out that the text says the cowardly, the unbelieving, the vile, murders, sexual immoral, those who practice magic arts, idolaters, and all liars will not be in Heaven. He then offered assurance to his listeners. "There may have been times in our lives when we were guilty of one or more of those transgressions, but absolutely no one needs to be eliminated. It is all about *guilt* and through Jesus all guilt can be removed. We who were once sinners can be as if we have never sinned." The people in the pews seemed to be transported to the very streets of the New Jerusalem during Davis' twenty-five minute presentation.

The message was closed with Davis making a suggestion. "I don't know about you, but this place called Heaven sure sounds to me like the best possible destination. I decided some years ago that it was the place for me when this life is over. I made my reservations when I was a teenager. Perhaps you need to make yours today. You can do so before we end this service. And the amazing fact is those reservations are free to us. Verse six of our text declares, 'I will give to drink without cost the spring of living water.' It is free because Jesus has already paid the cost! He did that at a place called Calvary."

After the service the guest speaker was asked to stand at the back door, as is the custom in many small country churches. He was appreciative of the handshakes and the comments he received. Several Crown Creek members suggested that he should agree to be a candidate for their open pulpit. He knew those who told him he should be preaching every Sunday meant well, but such comments just added to his feelings of guilt.

Davis joined Dean and Sherrie along with Al and his wife, Marsha for lunch at a restaurant east of town near the interstate ramp while Amy and Deidre made their way to Cartersville for a previously planned outing. Among other things, those at the table which the friendly waitress described as the noisiest in the restaurant discussed Davis' message. Al informed the group, "Before today I don't believe I had heard a sermon about Heaven since I was a boy about ten years of age."

"We are more likely to hear about Hell at our church", Dean spoke up.

"You don't go to church enough to know what the preacher's messages are about", Sherrie shot back.

"You may be right, but I'm going to do better in the future", he told his wife. "I think I would rather go to the place Davis described today than to the alternative."

"I hope you mean that. It is no fun sitting in church alone. Besides, I think it would probably do you a world of good to be in church each Sunday."

"You have done a good day's work with that sermon if it helps Sherrie get Dean back in church regularly." Al laughed as he turned toward Davis.

"I live to serve," Davis responded with a phrase he often heard his daughter use. "I sure wish I could get his brother Charley interested in spiritual matters."

"Charley is alright. He just needs to sow his wild oats," Dean defended his younger brother. "He is still young."

"You are right! He is a great guy. I don't know a better young man, but it is not about goodness. None of us are sufficiently good. That is the very reason we need Jesus."

"Give him time and he'll get it right," Dean argued.

Davis countered, "His job is extremely dangerous even here in our 'quiet' little town. I would feel better about him if he already had it right." After getting home Davis, tired from receiving little sleep the previous night, took the first Sunday afternoon nap he had taken in months. It was some of the most peaceful rest he had experienced in a while. When he awoke he thought, *it almost seems like I am back in the ministry, only Julie isn't here!*

Amy and Deidre got a quick lunch at a fast food restaurant on the out skirts of town before starting their short trek to Cartersville where they planned to attend a special event at the Booth Western Art Museum. Bartow County is fortunate to be home of the largest museum of western art east of the Mississippi. Today two new exhibits would be opened. They would have opportunity to meet the two artists as well as view their art. It was a program the two ladies made plans to attend several weeks earlier before they knew Davis would be speaking at Crown Creek. The rather steep registration fee had already been paid so missing the event was not an option.

Amy who was driving asked her friend, "Well, today was the first time you have heard Dad speak publicly, what do you think?"

"He was marvelous," Deidre quickly responded. His conversational tone is easy to listen to. I liked his sincerity and I thought his presentation was Biblical, interesting and easy to follow. He was obviously well prepared despite accepting the invitation on short notice."

"Dad has a few sermons that require very little preparation. He has presented them often, thus he needs only to spend a few minutes reviewing before he is ready to present them; however, I do not remember hearing him present this one before. I think it was just something that was on his heart."

"Do you think he will ever go back to the ministry?" Deidre questioned.

"I don't know. He and Mom were a team. I think he feels he cannot do it without her. There is no doubt in my mind that his heart is still in ministry, but I think he needs to work some things out. Should he someday find the right partner, I believe he would be open to the idea of returning to the pulpit. The problem is I don't know if he will ever find a partner that will measure up in his eyes."

"How would you feel about him finding someone," Deidre inquired.

"I loved my mother; no one can ever replace her, but I would be thrilled if someday Dad found that person that would make him happy."

"Is he serious about Tracie?"

Amy did a double take. *Why is she so inquisitive? Is Deidre interested in Dad? Surely not, there must be at least seventeen years age difference. ...But they would be a good match,* she determined as she quickly pondered the possibility before responding to Deidre's question.

"I don't really think so. He is lonely and he enjoys her companionship, but I doubt that it would ever go beyond that. I don't know her very well, but my observation is that despite her beauty and personality he could never be serious about her. She seems so shallow and worldly, just not the kind of woman with whom I see my Dad spending the rest of his life."

"I'm glad to hear you say that. I don't know what it is, but I have some serious questions about that woman. I am not sure she is the right one for him."

Again, Amy looked at her roommate in a new light. *How would I feel about Deidre and Dad? No, it is not going to happen,* she told herself as she pulled into the crowded parking lot. *Still....*

Tracie loved Sunday afternoons. She sat on the new over stuffed blue sofa in the living room with both feet tucked under her holding a cup of coffee in her right hand while listening to the soft music being piped through the house. *I should have gone to hear Davis speak*, she scolded herself. *I don't know why I find that kind of environment so uncomfortable. No doubt the Ross girl was there hanging on every word with that adoring look. Poor Davis, he is so naïve. He is completely ignorant of how that girl feels about him. Oh, well. It really doesn't matter.*

Tracie's thoughts went to the little church where Davis had spoken today. The Crown Creek church was the very one to which her grandparents had dragged her when she was a child. In her teen years she went only when forced, but enough to know she didn't want any part of what they had to offer. The back woods church was able to pull the wool over the eyes of her grandparents, but not her. How many times had Grandpa put his last dollar in the collection plate when he and Gram hardly had food to eat? More than twenty years had passed since Tracie had been inside any place of worship. She had to admit that she had enjoyed every thing about that day. The occasion was her wedding, her marriage to Tim. What a grand event it had been, everything she had dreamed of. It was too bad the marriage had not turned out to be as satisfying as the ceremony had been.

Tracie grew up on the edge of poverty. With beauty and personality she managed to cover that well during her teen years. With the help of student loans she attended the University for a couple of years, long enough to find and marry the man who would provide her what she needed. Her worst fear was that something would happen that would require her to return to the pay check to pay check existence that her parents had endured. She would do anything to keep that from happening. Tracie looked around her; large house, new furniture, expensive art work on the walls, three new cars in the garage, and people ready to do whatever she told them to do. Life is good she decided. She had just about everything she wanted and what she didn't yet have she would find a way to get. Maybe Davis and the primitive people at the Crown Creek church would frown on such a materialistic approach to life, but that didn't matter to Tracie. She knew what she wanted and she would get it! There was no one who would keep her from realizing her dreams.

Chapter 13

It was late Sunday afternoon after Davis finished his nap that his time with the Sunday paper was interrupted by the ring of the telephone. He got to the phone by the second ring. "Hello."

"Davis, this is Charley. The chief just called me with some information I thought you would want to know. They found Mr. Brown's car about noon today in the wooded area down by the water works on old 140. He was inside the wreck dead. The chief said it looked like he tried to take the curve too fast. It probably happened last night, but hardly anyone uses that old road since the new one opened. I guess that accounts for no one finding him until today. It was one of our officers, Eddie Jackson, who happened to notice the tire tracks and torn up turf on the hillside. When he got out to investigate, he spotted the demolished automobile buried deep in the bushes."

"Do you really think it was an accident, Charley?"

"Not for a moment!"

"Why do you suppose the killers tried to make it look like an accident this time? They didn't bother to cover up Ed's murder. When they tried to kill me, they didn't seem to care that the world knew it was murder. Of course, I'm assuming Brown was killed by the same men."

"They were probably sure that Ed's murder or your murder would provide no clues to their identity; however, if Mr. Brown is murdered causing us to launch an all out investigation, we will likely discover why he was here. That could lead us to them. If it is an accident with no serious investigation following the apparent mishap, they are safe."

"Do you think the chief will assume murder, or will he buy accident?"

"Right now he seems to be working under the assumption that it was an accident."

"I assume that means the next of kin will be contacted, arrangements will be made immediately to get the body back to Boston, and no autopsy will be done."

"That's about the size of it," Charley said. "That is, if the chief decides nothing fishy went on. By the way, you know what this means?"

It took Davis only a moment to answer. "It means those guys are not running. They are still in the area. They cannot afford to allow someone who can identify them to walk around. They will probably try to complete what they started."

"You pretty much hit the nail on the head. You better keep your guard up twenty-four seven."

"Thanks for calling Charley. Don't you ever call with good news?"

"Maybe one day I'll be able to call to tell you we've solved the case and have the bad guys behind bars."

"I hope that will be soon. My life sure is getting complicated."

Knowing "the rat faced" man and his partner were still in town, Davis was mindful of every person he saw on the road when he drove to church that evening. The evening worship experience did seem to calm his nerves a bit. John's sermon, entitled *Coming Home*, based on the parable of the Prodigal Son, was thought provoking enough to get Davis' mind off his troubles at least for a time.

Amy and Deidre had Monday off for Memorial Day. Amy, having appointments with a wedding consultant and a photographer, drove to Rome. Deidre chose not to go, probably because she still had not gotten over the hurt and disappointment of her own canceled plans almost a year earlier. Davis' exhaustion caught up with him which led to a decent Sunday night's sleep despite his Sunday afternoon nap. He got up over an hour later than usual. He showered, deciding not to shave today since no customers would be in his closed shop even if he decided to go there. Shaving was a daily chore he despised. He took advantage of any opportunity to by-pass the ritual often toying with the idea of growing a beard. He put on jeans, a Braves tee shirt, and sneakers before walking down the hall way to the front porch to retrieve the morning paper. Returning to the kitchen Davis put bread in the toaster; he sat down with a cup of coffee which was a little stronger than he liked it reading the front page before turning to the sports section of his paper. Davis then decided a few minutes on his exercise bike were needed. Twenty minutes going almost full speed was as much as he could handle on this particular day.

Later in the morning his mind clear from the night's sleep, Davis tried to piece together the events of the past few weeks. What could Ed have wanted to show him? Apparently whatever it was had been destroyed in the explosion. How was he an inconvenience and to whom? He was not aware of one single enemy in his hometown. And how does his being an inconvenience tie in with Ed Hagan? He hardly knew the man. The only tie between him and Ed was that Ed had worked a few days for him. Most of the work had been done before Davis arrived from Indiana.

His pondering produced no results, so facing a dead line he eventually turned to working on his "As I Remember It" column. He enjoyed putting together the piece about a young science teacher fresh out of college. Davis grinned to himself as he worked at the keyboard remembering how he, a high school junior, was quite taken with the beautiful young teacher. Amy and Deidre's classes must be full of smitten young men he guessed. It thrilled Davis that Miss Ralston seemed to like him choosing him for special tasks such as the time she asked him to help her with the load of materials she needed to carry home. She was cheerleader sponsor which, to his delight, meant she was present at all football and basketball games. In a basketball game in Rockmart, he was called for traveling. Disagreeing with the call, he turned to the official chiding, "O come on ref!" The referee was quick on the trigger, calling a technical foul on him, a call normally reserved for much stronger language or when unacceptable behavior was in evidence.

Later that evening, as players, coaches, and cheerleaders filed off the bus, Miss Ralston sought him out scolding, "Davis, I am very disappointed in you." He stood speechless. She was well on her way home before he realized she thought he had cursed the official or worse. His shyness kept him from ever telling her the true story. She married some lucky guy moving to Florida a year later. Her memory of him, no doubt, tarnished forever. Davis closed the column with a plea. "Miss Ralston, wherever you are now, please believe me, I'm not guilty." Davis appropriately entitled the piece, *Not Guilty.*

Writing about his high school days reminded Davis of Tracie. He tried to call her, but got her answering service. "Tracie, this is Davis. I didn't want anything in particular. I've missed you. I'll call you later." He sat down trying to read an Agatha Christie mystery novel he brought home from his shop, but found it extremely difficult to concentrate. A knock came from his front door. When he opened the door, he saw Deidre looking lovely in a very natural kind of way dressed in jeans and a navy blue tee shirt. He liked her dark hair as it was now, down rather than pulled back.

"I am getting ready to make a sandwich. I have a salad and iced tea. I hate to eat alone," she declared. "Would you like to join me for lunch?"

"I would be delighted to join you for lunch, Deidre." He responded with a smile. "I was just thinking that I probably didn't have anything in the house fit to eat. I thought I would have to go out for a burger, but I much prefer joining you." Davis waved at the officer in the patrol car standing guard in front of the house as he walked around the corner to the apartment on the opposite side of his quarters. "That must be the most boring duty in the world." Davis looked toward the officer who straightened his posture from the slumped position in which he sat before he noticed them looking his way. Maybe we could take him a sandwich," he suggested to Deidre.

"That's a good idea," she concurred.

Davis saw a lot of Deidre since she was Amy's roommate, but despite that and the fact she lived next door, he actually knew very little about her past. He had not realized that before Charley asked him about her.

"Tell me a little about yourself, Deidre. Who is Deidre Ross?"

"She looked at Davis with a blank expression on her face. I'm not sure I know who she is other than a social studies teacher. There really isn't much to tell. Dad and Mom divorced when I was nine. I grew up convinced the two people I loved most hated each other. My mom worked in a shoe factory through most of my childhood. Dad, who was an auto body shop laborer, contributed very little toward our livelihood, but I was able to be with him on a regular basis. After high school I went to the University of Georgia in Athens determined that I would not live like my mom has had to live. I thought an education would insure me against poverty, but boy was I wrong about that. I want more in life, but I'm not sure exactly what I want, other than to be the best teacher I can be right now."

"I've never sat in one of your classes, but I would bet you are a fantastic teacher. You have all the qualities that I have always felt a teacher needed in order to be successful. I have wondered about the circumstances that brought you to our town?"

Deidre was silent for a moment as she reflected. "After my break-up with my fiancé, Jeff, I wanted to get away from Atlanta, but I did not want to go too far. I did my homework, finding that all three of the Bartow County high schools had teaching vacancies. I applied to each, and here I am. I knew about Adairsville because my grandmother spoke of it from time to time."

"What connection did your grandmother have with Adairsville?"

"I've never told anyone else this," her voice sounded reluctant. "I haven't even told Amy, but my family, a couple of generations back, lived here, the best I can tell south of town not too far from this very spot."

"Really? Why is it such a big secret?" Davis asked between bites of his ham sandwich.

"It's not actually a secret. I just find it hard to talk about. It has only been in the last few years that I got the whole story. The bottom line is that my great grandparents moved the family to South Georgia when their daughter, my grandmother, got pregnant in her young teens. I guess in those days, it was easier to run away from such things than to stay and face the music. She married my grandfather when she was only seventeen. They were married for over sixty years before his death."

"I suspect they had a good life together," Davis surmised.

"They did. They had to work hard all of their lives. They never had much financial security, but despite that they seemed always to be extremely happy. Both became devoted Christians as young adults eventually becoming pillars of their church. I think that was the key factor in their finding contentment."

"I'm glad to hear that," Davis added. "It is obvious that not everybody is going to be rich, but everybody can have a good and productive existence especially when they love the Lord. I've always felt that we choose what life will be for us. It is choice and not circumstance that determines the quality of our time on this earth. The most important choice, of course, is to follow the Lord."

"I've never thought of it exactly that way, but I suppose you are right at least to a degree."

"Sure I am. Have you ever known me to be wrong? I'd just as soon you didn't answer that question," he hastily added with a laugh.

"One thing is for sure," Deidre stated. "It is not difficult to find out about Davis Morgan, not around here. Everybody in this town knows and admires him. Raised by a mother who was loved by all, captain of his high school basketball and football teams, well educated with a Master's degree and work toward a Ph.D., respected preacher for more than twenty years, and now a successful business man and writer."

"It all sounds fantastic when you state it that way, but it is not that cut and dry. If you check the won-lose records of those high school teams on which I played, my being captain will not impress you very much. I've never been quite sure how to measure success in the ministry, and the verdict is still out on the business and writing ventures. Evidently there is someone who is not very impressed with me since he or she is trying to have me killed. Everything is not always as peachy as it seems, but I have to admit for the most part it has been a great ride up to this point, at least up until the last year or so." I think that has been due more to the people God has placed in my life than to achievements or accomplishments."

"Nevertheless, it is good to be admired, and I hope someday to be as well thought of by people around here as you are."

"There is no doubt in my mind that you are well on your way. I know one person who is a great fan or yours, and I'm becoming more so all the time."

Deidre patted his hand which was lying on the table with her own. "Thanks, I needed a pep talk. I suppose at times I am prone to get a little down on myself."

"There is absolutely no logical reason why you should," he assured her. "You've got as much going for you as anybody I know. After a few more minutes of conversation which Davis thoroughly enjoyed, he reluctantly got up from the table. "Well, it's time we close this meeting of the mutual admiration society. Can I help you clean the table?"

"It will only take me about two minutes. I'll make a couple of sandwiches and pour a glass of iced tea for our friend outside and let you take it to him. Then you can get back to whatever you were doing."

Davis spent the remainder of the day attempting to relax with his book. He had a hard time keeping his mind off Deidre. She was such a delightful young lady. He wondered why some fine young man had not long ago made her his bride. He found himself thinking he was glad that had not happened. He then decided he ought to be ashamed of himself. He had no right to have such feelings. Davis heard Amy's car pulling into the drive way about four thirty. In recent days he had breathed a little easier when he knew she was safe in her nest next door.

Passing up dinner Davis snacked throughout the evening allowing his thoughts to go back to happier times spent with Julie. He fell asleep in his recliner not waking until after midnight. He got up making his way to his bedroom, but by then he was wide awake. He lay in his bed unable to get back to sleep until almost time to get up.

Chapter 14

Things were in a tizzy almost all morning at the Adairsville Police station. It started when Jerry Stewart came by to report the strange activity at the old run down farm house up the road from him in the little isolated community of Pleasant Valley. "Those two hard cases are unloading stuff off that truck day and night," Jerry told the Chief. "They threatened my boy yesterday when he and his dog wandered into their yard. The boy said he saw a gun. They are going to hurt someone if you don't get out there soon."

The Chief had an officer check with the owner of the rental property where the two suspicious characters were living. It was learned they came there a little more than three months earlier claiming they were from Atlanta. They temporarily leased the property for six months with cash payment for the entire period being made at that time. The Chief immediately went to Cartersville for a search warrant. Before he left two policemen were posted on the hillside near the old farm house with instructions to stay out of sight immediately contacting the dispatcher when the two men returned. The Chief was convinced he had found Ed Hagan's killers and knew it would be to his credit if his department made the bust. The Adairsville Police Department shared jurisdiction in the Pleasant Valley area with the county Sheriff's Department; however, neither county nor state law enforcement departments were brought in.

One member of the surveillance team called a few minutes earlier to report the suspects had returned. Now there was a convoy of police cars crossing highway 41 headed for Pleasant Valley. The department owned seven patrol cars; five of them were now occupied by two officers each. Some of those officers usually worked other shifts, but all available people were called in for this operation. These men were dangerous. They would need all the manpower they could get! Charley drove the lead vehicle with Chief Hanson riding in the passenger seat beside him. He wondered, *is the Chief making too much of this? Whatever is going on out there is probably not good, but I don't know that these guys are professional killers. Oh well, better to be safe than sorry I suppose.*

The dilapidated structure that was their target sat perhaps one-eighth of a mile off of the narrow county road, hidden by a hill and trees that stood between the house and road. Patrol cars were parked with all ten policemen cautiously moving on foot toward the place where their marks were assumed to be. After a couple of minutes the two officers already on site joined them. As they approached the house, the Chief quietly instructed his men to spread out, sending Charley and three others to the back of the house to cover the back door. When Charley and his crew were in place, he heard the voice of the Chief. "This is Chief Hanson from the Adairsville Police Department. Open your front door please. We need to talk with you."

There was perhaps a minute of silence before two men both in white t-shirts and jeans burst out the back door running full speed toward the heavy woods behind the house. Charley with his gun in hand yelled. "Stop or we will be forced to shoot!" Neither man slowed down. Charley yelled again, but it didn't stop the two crooks trying to get to the wooded area. Not seeing any guns in the hands of the runners, Charley quickly put his own gun back in the holster and started running toward one of the fugitives while yelling back to the other three cops, "I'll get this one!" It didn't take the young policeman, who had been a sprinter on his high school track team, long to reach the obviously out of shape thug in front of him. When Charley got within about three feet of the fleeing figure, he left his feet making a tackle that would have made his football star brother, Dean, proud. The fugitive laying on the ground trying to get his breath did not attempt to get up or fight off the policeman. In a moment or two Charley and his captive were surrounded by three policemen all with their guns drawn. Charley got to his feet, helped the man in the white t-shirt get off the ground before cuffing him. He immediately spotted the other fugitive already cuffed being escorted by several policemen.

When they went into the house, they found two rifles and several hand guns, but little furniture other than a sofa and a chair in the front room and two beds in one of the bedrooms; however, they were hardly able to walk through the five rooms for all the clutter. Electronics seemed to be the prevailing theme. The rooms were filled with computers, monitors, printers, televisions, stereo equipment, and gadgets Charley didn't even recognize. Out in the old barn behind the house they found kitchen appliances, furniture which was mostly antique, lawn mowers and much more. "I don't know if we have our killers, but we certainly have the thieves who have been terrorizing northwest Georgia over the past few weeks." Charley remarked to one of his fellow officers.

When the uniformed posse returned to the station the two prisoners were booked and secured. Chief Hanson instructed Charley, "Go down to the bookshop and see if Morgan is there. Bring him back here. Let's see if he can identify these turkeys."

Following orders Charley walked to the Stock Exchange where he found Davis with a customer. After Davis finished helping the gentleman find a book about fishing, Charley approached him with a grin. "Don't get too excited, but we have two thieves in our jail that the Chief thinks could be our murderers. He wants you to come down to the jail with me to see if you can identify them."

Immediately Davis came alive with the news. "Does either of them look like a rat?" He excitedly asked his young friend.

"If you ask me they both look like rats," Charley replied.

Davis was hopeful as he rapidly walked with Charley to the jail. He had never seen so many uniforms in one place as were swarming the little police station on this day. Chief Hanson led him back to the jail cells pointing to the men behind the bars. "Have you ever seen these two before?" Both prisoners looked up at Davis.

In a split second the optimistic hope that had taken hold of Davis a few minutes earlier when Charley gave him the news was gone. "I have never seen either of those men," he told the anxious Chief.

The next question was predictable. "Are you sure?" The voice of the Chief was that of a dejected man.

"I am absolutely sure! Neither man looks even similar to the thugs who accosted me." Returning to his shop, Davis was glad the thieves had been captured, but he was sorely disappointed the dangerous killers were still at large.

There had been some hard days since Julie's body had been laid to rest in the East View Cemetery on the hill southeast of town, but Davis could not remember one more difficult than this one. It was exactly one year earlier that she passed away on her birthday. On his way to the grave site with flowers, Davis' mind went back to that time a year ago when Julie fought so hard to stay alive. Even though she was not conscious most of that day he still believed she had resisted death so diligently because it was her birthday. She did not want him and Amy to have to endure the memory of her passing on her birthday each year. When Davis got out of his car walking to the grave site, he saw that yellow roses were already lying against the head stone on the grave. Yellow roses were her favorite. He held a dozen of that very flower in his right hand. No doubt, Amy visited the grave site, leaving the roses before going to school this morning. Davis wasn't prone to tears. He was not usually an emotional man and did not cry easily, but his eyes clouded. He could feel the moisture running down both cheeks. After bending over to lay the roses on the grave along side those already there, he straightened up pulling out his handkerchief to wipe his eyes. Davis had never used profanity in his entire life, but at this moment he was overcome with the need to curse. He gave in to the temptation yelling a curse word not once, but three times. He was instantaneously ashamed of himself knowing that Julie would be sorely disappointed in him. If he had done such a thing in her presence, she would have calmly asked him, "Davis, do you really think that is going to do any good?" He decided such an outburst did not honor his deceased wife and it surely disappointed the Father. He silently asked the Lord's forgiveness for his lack of control.

Davis was convinced Julie was not in the grave that he now stood over. He repeated Paul's words from II Corinthians chapter five, verse eight that had become so important to him in the last year: "We are confident, I say, and would prefer to be away from the body and at home with the Lord." His head as well as his heart told him that Julie was away from the body and at home with the Lord. He knew that his wife had enjoyed living immensely, but he also understood that as good as life had been, she was better off now than she had ever been before. *But why did he so miss her? He ought to be able to let go and be happy for her.* He didn't know if he would ever be able to do that. He knew he was selfish, but despite recognizing his selfishness he still had not been able to overcome it. Over and over again he had promised Julie as he had promised the Lord that he would keep trying. He did try, but so far without success. Davis remembered some of the words he had used in an effort to comfort members of his churches when they had lost loved ones. He thought how ridiculously cliché he must have sounded to his grieving friends. Davis continued to believe it important to comfort those left behind, but his recent experience led him to the conclusion that the use of "words" was not the way to do it. He now understood a seminary professor's instructions when he said, "What you say is not as important as simply being there."

Caught up in his thoughts, Davis was a bit startled when the cell phone in his pocket rang. He took the phone out. Looking at the small screen in his hand he saw that it was Tracie. He spoke into the sometimes annoying object, "Hello Tracie."

"Davis Honey, I was thinking of you. I just thought I would check to see how your day is going..."

"I appreciate it, but I am not in a position to talk. I'll call you a little later."

"Okay, is there anything wrong? Can I do anything for you?"

"No", Davis responded rather curtly. "I will talk with you later."

Tracie's closing words were, "I love you".

Standing beside Julie's grave, Davis could not duplicate Tracie's words of affection. He simple said, "Goodbye Tracie", and closed his cell phone.

There was no logical reason why it should be hard to talk with Tracie while standing beside Julie's grave. There was no rationale for him feeling the guilt he now felt. He knew if he was ever to be content again he would need to get a handle on such unreasonable feelings. Davis spent another half hour at the grave site before getting back into the car. Before starting the engine he took out his cell phone punching Tracie's number. "Tracie, I am sorry for my rudeness. I'm just having a little bit of a rough day today..."

Believing there is great power in prayer, Deidre prayed for both Amy and Davis throughout the day. She knew that today was Amy's mother's birthday as well as the first anniversary of her death. Amy had mentioned that fact as they ate dinner last night. When Deidre came out of her bedroom this morning Amy was already gone. The yellow roses she had purchased were also missing. She guessed Amy went to her Mom's grave to deliver the flowers. As much as Amy had struggled in the early weeks after her Mom's death, she seemed to have successfully gone through the grief process now recovering well. She suspected that Jay had a lot to do with that. Regardless of the progress Amy had made, today would be a rough day for the young woman of which she had come to think of as a younger sister.

It was a different story for Amy's dad. He tried desperately to conceal his hurt, but failed miserably at the effort. She guessed that the kind of day Amy was experiencing today was a daily routine for Davis, but today would be even worst for him. Deidre wished she had the nerve to speak to Davis about his unresolved loss, but who was she to counsel such a man. She decided she might not be able to speak to him about his struggles, but she could certainly continue to pray. She intended to do that for as long as she felt there was a need to do so. Davis had as much to offer as any man she knew, but his usefulness would be severely hampered until he got on top of his own problems. *Lord, show me what I can do to help him*…

Chapter 15

"I thought I would let you know, Mr. Brown's body is being flown back to Boston later today. The chief has ruled it an accident." Charley telephoned Davis with the news.

"Do you have time off anytime soon?" Davis inquired.

"My schedule calls for four days off starting on Thursday. Why do you ask?"

"How would you like to take an all expenses paid trip to Boston?"

"I've never been to Boston. I always did want to visit the East. Free would certainly be the way to go."

"I'll see if I can make flight, car rental and motel arrangements for us. Pack for a four day trip. Plan to be ready on Thursday. Can you get the name and address of Mr. Brown's next of kin without alerting the chief?"

"That shouldn't be a problem."

"Even though my best body guard will be with me, I'd feel safer if we didn't advertise where we are going. I'll probably tell only Amy, Deidre, and Tracie. I would suggest we keep it as quiet as possible."

"I think that is wise. Let me know about the arrangements when you complete them."

Reservations were made for an early Thursday morning Delta flight. Davis was looking forward to the trip not only because it enabled him to feel he was doing something positive toward solving his own problems, but also because the Boston area was one of his favorite places. It would be his first trip back since he and Julie last vacationed there three summers ago. It was then that he met Wyman, his doctor-bookseller friend. Cape Cod, just an hour from the city of Boston, had been a favorite vacation spot for Davis' family for years. Sometimes Amy would be with them, but often after she reached her middle teens, the trips would be alone times for Julie and himself. Returning there without her would no doubt seem strange.

"I appreciate you paying travel expenses," Charley told him while they were in flight.

"No problem. The trip is for my benefit. Besides, I can afford it. I made an eight thousand dollar sale awhile back," Davis told his friend.

"Are you telling me you sold a single book for eight grand?" Charley's mouth dropped open in disbelief.

"That is what I am saying." Davis was amused at the young policeman's reaction.

"I didn't know books existed with that kind of value."

"Some are worth a great deal more than that, but they are not easy to find. I don't have them everyday."

"I doubt anyone in Adairsville would pay over twenty-five dollars. How are you going to move them even if you find them?"

"You'd be surprised. However, you are right. Most of the real money customers are serious collectors and dealers out of Atlanta and Chattanooga plus what I do on the internet."

"What do you mean by serious collectors? How is a collector different from a serious collector?"

"A collector may be someone who collects a particular author or perhaps is interested in a particular subject. He may not care whether or not it is a first edition or if it is in top-notch condition as long as it is readable and in acceptable shape. Such a person is collecting for the content. He is likely to read the books in his collection, sometimes over and over. On the other hand, the serious collector wants a first edition as close to the condition in which it was issued as possible. He is buying the book to have it not read it. He probably would buy a cheap copy to read if he were inclined to read it at all."

"That doesn't make a lot of sense to me," Charley looked confused. "I thought books were made to read."

"Collectors of anything rarely make sense. There are several kinds of used and out of print bookstores. There are reader's stores, collector's stores, and stores that cater to the serious collector," he explained.

"Which kind is yours?"

"I would describe it as a collector's store with some stock for the serious collector."

"I suppose a book has to be old in order to be worth anything?" The young police officer asked.

"No, that is not always true. I recently sold a first edition of James Lee Burke's first book published, I believe, in 1965 for more than a thousand dollars. First editions of To Kill a Mocking Bird in collector's condition are now worth more than four thousand dollars and sometimes bring as much as six thousand. It was not published until 1960."

"Amazing," Charley said. "I guess there is a lot I don't understand about business. I think I'll stick to law enforcement."

"Someone once advised me, 'Don't work for a living. Do what you would do for free, but do it so well people will pay you to do it.' I think that's pretty good advice."

"Makes sense to me," Charley said. Tired of all the talk of books, he leaned his head back on the head rest closing his eyes hoping Davis would take the hint. The two friends remained relatively quiet napping for the remainder of the flight. Upon arrival in Boston, the two Georgians picked up their rental car after a short shuttle bus ride. Davis drove the rental with Charley complaining about the cramped conditions in the compact model Davis had reserved.

"It's all I can afford," Davis told him. "I almost always reserve a compact hoping they will not have one. When they don't have what has been reserved, the agency will upgrade to a larger model for the same price as the compact. Sometimes my strategy back fires leaving me with what I reserve."

"I thought you sold an eight thousand dollar book," he shot back.

"Eight thousand dollars won't last forever, especially in Boston."

They checked into their motel, just south of the city. "I guess you are going to complain because I didn't get us a room at the most luxurious hotel in the city," Davis suggested.

"No, this will do just fine," he said with a smile on his face noticing the two attractive young ladies coming toward them. They returned Charley's smile.

"I think you need to keep your mind on the reason we are here."

"I don't know why you are here, but I am keeping my mind on the reason I'm here," he laughed.

"Spare me," Davis responded. "If you start playing Romeo with these Boston girls you can expect to get shot down pretty quickly."

"You underestimate my southern charm," he joshed. "Beautiful girls are about the same anywhere. I know girls even better than you know books."

After delivering their luggage to their room, the two travelers set out to locate Mrs. Brown. They had an address, but had to stop at a convenience store for a city map in order to locate the street on which she lived. Davis gave Charley the map. "You navigate and I'll drive."

After getting lost several times, driving at least five miles out of their way, they finally found the Brown home in a well kept middle class neighborhood. Davis dreaded confronting Mrs. Brown. He reasoned that this was probably the day after the funeral. It's even possible; he calculated that the funeral was today. As cold as their intrusion would seem, it had to be done. That was why they were here.

A middle aged graying woman conservatively dressed who might be described as a bit heavy set came to the door after a few moments when Davis rang the door bell. "May I help you?" she asked with a pleasant voice, but with a look of sadness in her eyes. She spoke without opening the screen door.

"We are looking for Mrs. Brown."

"I'm Jane Brown."

"Mrs. Brown, I am Davis Morgan from Adairsville, Georgia, and this," he said motioning toward Charley, "is Charley Nelson an Adairsville police officer." Charlie identified himself by silently pulling his credentials from his pocket showing them to the widow. "We are sorry to intrude at what I know is a difficult time for you, but we are investigating your husband's death. There are some questions we have traveled all the way from Georgia to ask you. I assure you we will take only a moment of your time." He made the promise feeling extremely self-conscious about being there.

"I was told that my husband's death was due to an automobile accident." She responded apparently surprised by the implication of anything to the contrary.

"That is the official position right now, and it may very well be fact, but Mr. Morgan and I want to make sure. Anytime an investigator dies a red flag goes up," Charley told her.

Opening the door, she invited them into the well kept living room where they were seated on a sofa facing their hostess who took her place in a large chair. "Do you have any idea what your husband was working on in Adairsville, Mrs. Brown?" Davis asked.

"No, I don't. I assume it was the usual legal matter. He never told me much about his cases while he was working on them. Sometimes after the fact, he would get talkative about his experiences if anything unusual happened, but seldom in the midst of an investigation. This job seemed to me rather routine, nothing out of the ordinary. Whatever it was, he was about to close it out."

"Why do you say that?" Davis nudged.

"He called me the day of his death to tell me he would probably be home in a couple of days," Jane Brown revealed. "He had already made flight arrangements to get home."

"Did he give you any reason to believe what he was doing was dangerous?" Charley inquired.

"No more than usual. Sherman's cases were not normally very dangerous. Even though he had a permit for a gun, most of the time that gun remained in a dresser drawer here in our bedroom."

"Did he take the gun with him to Adairsville?" Charley questioned.

"No", the lady responded. "It is still in the dresser drawer."

Davis asked. "Did he mention any names connected to the case?"

"I only remember one," she told them. "Let's see if I can remember," she said pausing for a moment and shutting her eyes as if in thought. "He said something like… 'I think I have solved the mystery of Dixie Adair.' Yes, that was it, Dixie Adair," she repeated. "I remembered it because I thought it sounded so Southern." Does that make sense?"

"I'm sure it will help us get to the bottom of this," Charley told her. "I understand there were several law firms your husband worked for regularly. Do you know with which one he was working on the Georgia case?"

"If I'm not mistaken, it was Raymond Camp's firm."

"Do you know where Mr. Camp's office is located?" Davis asked.

"I know it's somewhere on the Cape. I think Hyannis Port."

Charley wrote the information on a small pad.

"One more thing and we will get out of your hair," Davis said. "Your husband had made an appointment to talk with me on the night he died. When you spoke with him earlier that day, did he give you any hint as to what he wanted to tell me?"

108

"No he didn't. I'm sure he never mentioned your name. The only thing he said about the case was that "Dixie Adair" statement." She assured them.

"You've been very helpful," Davis said rising to walk toward the door. "We appreciate your willingness to speak to us even though we are a couple of strangers."

"Will you keep me informed?" she requested.

"Yes, ma'am, we will," Charley told her. "Our investigation is unofficial, but we will sure let you know if we find that your husband's death was anything other than an accident."

As he got to the door, Davis turned speaking again to the grieving widow. It was true he had lost faith in the ability of *words* to comfort, but he felt the need to reach out to Mrs. Brown in some way. "I understand that you don't know me, Mrs. Brown. Nothing I can say is going to help you much, but I want you to know I to have had to deal with what you are going through. It hasn't been very long since I lost my wife. At first I didn't think there was any way I could get through it. I will not tell you that time will take care of the hurt, but I do want you to know that I am coping better now than six months ago. I believe for me, the healing started with the realization that my Father in Heaven is willing to step in where I am not capable. I do not know if you are a Christian, Mrs. Brown, but I want you to know that God loves you and wants to help you through this. I encourage you to let Him do so. I recall an account in the Bible when Jesus and his disciples were in a boat when a storm occurred. Jesus, perhaps with out stretched arms, spoke the words 'Peace be still.' Immediately there was calmness, winds ceased and waves became normal. I assure you that Jesus can speak those same words to your heart, 'peace be still' and you can experience a calm that will enable you to face the future with confidence." Davis certainly believed the words he had spoken, but still felt a little like a hypocrite when they came out of his mouth. "Practicing what you preach" was the phrase that came to his mind.

Fighting hard to hold back the tears that were forming in her eyes, Mrs. Brown took both his hands managing to say, "Thank you," in a voice filled with emotion.

Returning to the car, Davis hoped his effort was beneficial to Mrs. Brown for whom he was feeling real empathy. He knew that even a few days earlier he could not have offered such a positive reflection. He decided that must be evidence of at least some progress on his part. After riding in the direction from which they had come for four or five minutes in silence Charley asked, "Where to now?"

"It is too late for us to get to Mr. Camp's office today. I suggest we drive to the Cape first thing in the morning. We haven't had anything to eat today. I'm starting to get hungry. After we eat, we can go back to the motel and relax."

"*Dixie Adair*," Charley slowly repeated both words. "Do you know anyone by that name?"

"No, but I vaguely remember hearing something about a baby called that or something similar. I cannot recall the details. It happened way back even before my time. If I remember correctly, it involved an infant being found in a cemetery. I'm sure we will be able to find someone who knows the whole story when we get back home."

"Why would Mr. Brown be interested in a baby found so long ago in an Adairsville cemetery?"

"Maybe Lawyer Camp will be able to help us with that. I bet we can get a good steak over there." Davis was already turning into the restaurant parking lot. The steak was a little tough; nevertheless, the hungry Davis enjoyed the meal while Charley mostly complained.

Davis took a Boston newspaper with him back to the motel. Charley watched a movie on TV while Davis lay on one of the beds reading the sports page. It wasn't long before he was dosing, dropping the paper across his chest. When he awakened Charley was gone. It was starting to get dark outside. Davis got up pulling back the curtain covering the window to see if Charley had taken the car. The rental was where they had left it earlier. Charley must have walked to the motel lounge or to a nearby convenience store, or maybe he was just stretching his legs. More likely Davis thought, he was chasing an attractive young lady he had spotted somewhere. At that moment Davis caught a glimpse of a man across the parking lot moving quickly into the space between two of the motel units where the soft drink and ice machines were located.

At first he was startled thinking it might be the "rat faced man." *Don't be ridiculous*, he told himself. *There is no way it could be him, or could it?* He took a second look, but the figure was no longer in sight. Over the next few minutes he pushed the curtain back several times to take a quick look, but he saw no one but a child buying a soda.

Charley returned a few minutes later explaining he had remembered he needed razor blades. He had gone to purchase them. Davis said nothing about the suspicious figure near the vending machines. He was still drowsy from having just awakened when he saw the man, and besides he had been known to have an active imagination. There was not a chance it could be him, he reasoned, but he wondered. His uncertainty kept him awake much of the night.

Chapter 16

The six o'clock a.m. wake up call came as Davis requested just moments after the alarm he had set sounded. Davis never trusted his ability with electronic gadgets, thus the request for a wakeup call. Check out was handled with Charley grumbling about the early hour. Davis suggested they could spend the remainder of the day and Saturday on the Cape if they found no reason to return immediately to Boston. He explained to Charley, "We shouldn't have any problems finding a room even without reservations since tourist season doesn't start on the Cape until the first of July."

"That sounds fine to me. I'm just along for the ride."

"The badge doesn't hurt," laughed Davis.

Eating sausage, eggs, and toast with their coffee at the motel break-fast bar, they were in their little compact rental on the road heading south toward their destination by 7:30. Rush hour traffic wasn't a problem since they were leaving the city. Most of the traffic was coming in. In little more than an hour, they crossed the Bourne Bridge. There was something magic about crossing that bridge that always brought a feeling of excitement to Davis, as if he were leaving one world to enter another. He explained to Charley, "The Hyannis area is the commercial center of the Cape, which probably has something to do with it being geographically near the middle. I love the oldness of things in this part of the country," Davis told his friend. He pointed to a beautiful white church building with a tall steeple telling his companion, "that one dates from the seventeenth century."

"Why don't we have buildings that old down south?" Charley asked.

"This is where the country began, and, besides, General Sherman burned many of our older buildings back in eighteen sixty-four or was it sixty-five. That is one of the reasons older books are easier to find here than in Georgia. Many of them were destroyed when many southern houses and buildings were set on fire in the Civil War."

"Everything relates to your business, doesn't it?" Charley commented.

"That's what I do. I don't know a lot, but I know a little about books."

They located the office for the firm that included Raymond Camp, but not having an appointment, Davis and Charley spent a good deal of time in the lawyer's reception room before getting into his office. That didn't bother Charley too much since the receptionist was an attractive blond who liked Charley's Southern drawl. Davis had always hated waiting. Julie often reminded him that patience was a virtue. The hour and half they waited seemed more like three to the fidgety Davis. He was relieved when the receptionist finally announced as she smiled at Charley, "Mr. Camp will see you now."

"I'm Raymond Camp," the tall graying gentleman in the tailored blue suit said as he held his hand out to first Davis then Charley. Each man warmly shook his hand introducing himself.

"I understand you gentlemen are from Adairsville, Georgia, here about Brown's death I am told," He gave the impression that he was a busy man who wanted to get immediately to the business at hand so he could move on to that which he considered worthy of his time.

"That's right," Davis told him also wanting to keep things moving. "Mr. Brown called me the day of his death to make an appointment to talk about something he thought was tied to an attempt on my life. Do you know anything about that, Mr. Camp?"

"Absolutely nothing," he assured Davis. "The business I sent Sherman Brown to Georgia on is a simple legal matter. While he had not reported to me the results of his investigation, I cannot see how any violence could possibly be related to that assignment."

"Could you tell us more about it?" Charley inquired with his cop's interrogation tone.

"I'll tell you as much as I dare. You understand that I must respect my client's right to confidentiality. I am inclined to withhold names of those involved, unless it becomes necessary for me to reveal them."

"Just share with us what you feel you can ethically tell us," Davis suggested.

"I sent Brown to Georgia to search for someone who may or may not exist. I got involved in this around five years ago as the attorney for a very wealthy business man who passed away well past his ninetieth birthday. He had no immediate family or so it seemed. He outlived two wives, but had children with neither of them. I'll not tell you how the man made his money, since that would probably be the clue that would enable you to put a name with the story." The lawyer paused.

"Go on," Charley spoke.

"Conservatively speaking, my client left a fortune of at least half a billion dollars in tangible assets."

"Wow, that's a lot of money," Charley whistled. "But what does it have to do with Mr. Brown being in Adairsville?"

"It's a rather long and complicated story, but let me see if I can condense it. In his younger days the old man was somewhat of a ladies' man. While in his late teens, he spent several months on a plantation near Adairsville, Georgia with a friend of his family. It seems he gave most of that time to keeping company with your Southern belles. During the weeks he was there he was responsible for one and possibly two young ladies...," Mr. Camp paused. "How would you delicately say it down South? ...getting in a family way? He was aware of one of the children from the beginning. He never contacted mother or child, but he was aware of the child. He was told by the other girl that she was pregnant, but he never knew if it was indeed true. If she had a baby he was unaware of it. My client outlived his child's mother as well as his child, but there is one grandchild," the lawyer explained.

"But if the grandchild can be identified, what was your investigator doing in Adairsville?" Davis asked.

"He was there trying to determine if my client had a son or daughter by the second girl mentioned. You see, there was a stipulation in his will. Half of the estate went outright to the known grandchild. If it is proven by the seventh year after his death that he had another child, that person, or surviving descendants will receive the balance of the inheritance. If no such descendants are uncovered or survive, the known grandchild will receive the remainder of the estate on the seventh anniversary of my client's death. Sherman Brown was in Georgia because we are approximately two years away from the seventh year. I felt I owed it to my client and any other family members he may have to do everything possible to find the truth before the dead line."

"I don't suppose it would be possible for you to tell us the name of the known heir?" Davis asked, pretty sure of what the answer would be.

"No, I do not think that would be ethical, unless that individual gave me permission to release the name."

"Could you tell us if that person lives in Adairsville or elsewhere?" Charley inquired.

"I can't do that. You bring me evidence that this man or woman is somehow involved in something illegal relative to the situation with the will, and I will give you all the information I have; but, otherwise, I need to keep it confidential. My career is very closely related to my integrity."

"We understand that," Davis told him getting up to shake his hand. "I believe we are going to find the information you have given us helpful. We have taken up enough of your valuable time."

"There is one thing. Sherman Brown worked often for me. I knew him only professionally, but I knew him to be a good and honest family man, a Vietnam War hero. If there is any possibility that his death was anything other than an accident, you find whoever did it."

"We will do our best, Mr. Camp," Charley assured him.

Davis suggested they drive to Falmouth for no reason other than the fact it was his favorite spot on the Cape. "We shouldn't have a problem finding a place to spend the night there," he told Charley.

"Well, what do you make of Mr. Camp's story, Davis?" Charley asked, anxious to get his friend's input. "Do you think any of that information has anything to do with Ed's murder, the explosion, or the attempts on your life?"

"Evidently Mr. Brown thought so. It would certainly be to the advantage of the known descendant if no other surviving heir be found, He or she would stand to inherit an additional quarter of a billion dollars, but I don't know what that has to do with Ed or me."

"Maybe Ed was the heir or perhaps it's you?"

"That doesn't seem likely since Ed moved to Adairsville from southern Alabama less than twenty years ago with no previous ties to Adairsville. And as much as I would like to inherit all that money, the lineage on my father's side is very cut and dried with no possibility of the kind of thing Camp was talking about. My mother came to Adairsville as a foster child to live with the Walsh family when she was in her early teens with no Adairsville history. I can't see any connection. Brown did seem interested in my mother after he read my column about her. He might have mistakenly tied her into this mess."

"Maybe he wasn't mistaken at all. Perhaps he learned something you don't know about your family. That is certainly possible." Charley suggested.

"Maybe, but I cannot imagine what it would be. I don't know if it will help us to find out who the old man was, but that is something we might be able to learn. There is a good library in Falmouth. I would say the old man was a resident or at least a part time resident of the Cape since his lawyer is here. He died approximately five years ago. He was over ninety years of age and very rich. It should not be hard to identify him from the death announcements in the newspaper."

"Great idea," Charley responded. "You're starting to think like a policeman."

"Oh, I hope not," Davis kidded his friend.

They were told at the library that past issues of the local paper had been put on microfilm. Both men jumped into the task at hand. After almost two hours of looking through obituaries, Davis began to think that this idea was not going to pan out, when he heard Charley excitedly proclaim, "Here it is!"

"The old rich guy's name was Judson Reed," he told Davis. He was a member of one of the older local families who were once in the shipping business. It appears he inherited the family business as a young man, but lost everything in the late thirties. There were several business ventures through the years some mildly successful. In the mid nineteen fifties he bought an inn. By nineteen sixty-two he had turned that single inn into a chain of motels covering several New England states. Well respected for his business savvy, a member of several civic clubs and organizations and donor to several charities! Not much else here," Charley surmised. He moved out of the way so Davis could read the article.

Davis took his pen and a piece of scratch paper he had retrieved from the information desk to take some notes, but saw nothing he thought would help them, at least, not at this point.

It was mid-afternoon already, so they decided to skip lunch and feast on sea food at dinner time. It would show poor judgment to spend time on the cape while not taking advantage of the delicious sea food offered in its restaurants. "Let's find a room," Davis suggested. "Julie, Amy, and

I always stayed in a cottage we rented at a campground near one of the beaches which rents only by the week. I don't really know much about other lodging here. All we need are clean beds in which to sleep. That shouldn't be too difficult."

They drove through the village square area with its shops and early colonial churches. Davis could never drive or walk through the village without the word quaint coming to his mind. They turned toward the marina. Saltbox structures with blue shutters and flower boxes below the widows lined both sides of the shaded street reminding Davis of why he so loved the Cape. "We might be able to afford a room there," Davis said pointing to a nice series of buildings off to the right. "It is off-season so prices will be cheaper than later in the summer when the tourist will double the population."

Their inquiry revealed that there were indeed vacancies. Davis filled out the registration form, handed the clerk his Visa card taking the receipt and key card. Charley parked the car almost directly in front of their room. They took their luggage into their quarters. "Not bad." Charley carefully examined the nicely decorated room, a good deal larger than the one in which they had stayed the previous night.

"How is everything in Adairsville," Davis asked Amy after punching her number.

"About the same, you know things don't change here very much. I went to the post office and got your mail this morning. I've checked your answering machine a couple of times since you have been gone. There was nothing important at the post office or on the machine. Are you having a profitable trip?"

"I think so. We talked with Mrs. Brown as well as the lawyer for which her husband was working. We have gathered some information that we are still going to have to filter through. Tell Deidre I said hello. Ask her to do her best to keep you out of trouble while I am away," he instructed.

"I will tell her you said hello. Do you still plan to be back late Sunday?"

"Yeah, our flight arrives in Atlanta shortly after five, so we should be back in Adairsville by six-thirty or seven or maybe a little later. Wish you were here with us."

"I do too. How does Charlie like New England?" she asked.

"You know Charley. As long as there are beautiful women around, he can be happy anywhere," he laughed.

"I heard that!" Charley shouted from the across the room. "And everything you say is true."

Davis gave Amy the name of the motel with instructions on how to reach them. "Unless something comes up to change our minds we will be here both tonight and tomorrow night. Call me here or on my cell if you need me for any reason."

"I will," she assured him. "I love you. Be careful."

"I love you. Careful is my middle name. See you late Sunday."

"What's going on in Boston?" Deidre questioned her roommate after Amy placed the handset back in its place. "Have they found any answers?"

"It doesn't sound to me like they have made any earth shattering discoveries, but I think they are enjoying themselves. I am sure we will get a full report when they return. I feel a lot better knowing Charley is there with Dad. Until I learned he was going, I had some real reservations. I feared for Dad's safety."

Deidre had also been concerned, but not wanting to alarm Amy had said nothing to her roommate about her own fears. She had not had a good feeling about the trip from the beginning. There was nothing she could put her finger on, but in her mind there seemed to be a cloud hanging over the whole venture. Deidre had been praying for the safety of the two men on regular intervals every since they left home.

"I suspect one of Dad's motives for taking the trip was to simply get away for a few days. It seems to me that the information they are after could just as well have been gathered by phone or computer. You know that the Boston area, specifically Cape Cod, is just about Dad's favorite place this side of Heaven? It didn't surprise me one bit when Dad told me they were on the Cape."

"I didn't know he was so fond of that part of the country. Has he been there often?"

"When I was a child and even a teenager we went to Cape Cod for vacation about once every two years, sometimes more often than that. It got old for me. When I was in high school I would often beg off staying with a friend while Mom and Dad made the trip. I think they let me do that because they liked taking long walks on the beach together. They enjoyed the romantic dinners just the two of them could have without me tagging along. When Dad finds something he likes, it is hard to get him to alter that routine. That is true of food, recreation, vacations and just about every-thing else."

"It must have been neat growing up in an environment where your parents were so in love with one another." Deidre spoke more to herself than to Amy.

"Living with two parents like Mom and Dad has certainly given me goals for my own marriage. I think one of the big reasons I love Jay so much is that I see the same look in his eyes when he looks at me as I often saw in Dad's eyes when he looked at Mom. The down side is that when one of the two lovers is gone, the other is left devastated."

Tell me about it, Deidre said to herself. *Sometimes separation comes in ways other than death, but it is no less devastating.* Deidre silently prayed several times that evening for Davis and Charley's safety.

Before looking for a place where they could enjoy the sea food feast they were anticipating, Davis talked Charley into going with him to a nearby book store. He convinced his companion they would be there only a few minutes since it would be near closing time. The wonderful book stores scattered across the cape is just one more reason Davis so enjoyed being there. They had less than twenty minutes to browse in this one before closing time, but that allowed Davis enough time to find four books that would be useful to him with the customary twenty per cent dealer discount. Charley looked around, not surprisingly; he found nothing he wished to purchase. For dinner, the two travelers decided on a restaurant called, The Captain's Table. "I have never eaten there," Davis told his friend. "But I have been told the seafood is delicious." Both the service and the food was everything he had heard. Even Charley had no complaints.

"I really like the beach at this time of the evening as well as early in the morning," Davis told Charley. "I've never been one, much to the dismay of my family when we were on vacation, to lie on the beach, but I do enjoy walking on it early in the morning and just before dark. I prefer to listen to the roar of the waves without the distraction of a lot of people. I relish the briskness of the air in the evening, and it seems to me that the smell of salt in the air is heavier in the morning and evening than at other times of the day."

"The only beaches I've been to have been in Florida, Daytona and Panama City," Charley told him.

"I think I'm going to take a walk along the beach."

"I'll go with you," Charley announced. I'm sure I could find someone with whom I would rather walk, but, after all, I am suppose to be your body guard. I would probably never get a date with Amy's pretty roommate if anything happened to you."

They both went into their room for windbreakers before going to the beach. "I'm glad you told me to bring a jacket," Charley told him. "It sure gets cool in the evenings up here at this time of the year."

"I've known it to be downright cold," Davis said. He recalled the first time he was there with his family being completely surprised by the early June weather as they were tent camping totally unprepared for the drop in the temperature that came when the sun went down each evening.

From time to time the two men passed others sometimes couples holding hands, but for the most part the beach was deserted. Davis surprised himself when he thought how much he would like to introduce Deidre to Cape Cod. *Why Deidre and not Tracie?* He silently questioned himself. He decided it was probably because Tracie was a woman of the world. Most likely there was little she had not seen and experienced, while Deidre had lived a rather sheltered life. *It would be fun introducing her to new places and experiences.* That conclusion enabled Davis to be at ease with his thoughts about Deidre since it was for her benefit, not his own that he wished she was with him. In only minutes darkness had overtaken them. They turned back toward their motel. It was one of those peaceful evenings that were so much apart of Cape Cod life.

"Watch out!" Charley yelled throwing Davis hard onto the sand. Not more than thirty feet in front of them stood the frame of a man with gun raised in the classic position with the left hand balancing the right. Even in the near darkness Davis could see in the split second before the attacker started firing that it was the "rat faced" man.

Charley rolled away from Davis reaching under his jacket. Davis instead of staying on the ground as he would have done had there been time to think, raised up on one knee trying to get to his feet. Two shots rang out in succession. Davis felt a spot on his left rib cage burning. He fell to the ground staying very still.

Chapter 17

Charley stood raising his own gun to draw attention away from Davis, but the "rat faced" man fired first then turned and ran before Charley who had dropped to his knees could return fire. As the shooter disappeared Charley sank onto the sand. Davis tried to get to his feet. Charley shouted, "Stay down!"

"Thank You, Lord," Davis muttered. "He's still alive."

Davis waited a few moments before calling out. "Charley are you all right?"

"I'm hit, but I don't think it is anything serious. Can you see him?"

"I'm not sure, but I think he has gone."

"Don't take any chances, we may still be within his range," Charley instructed as Davis on hands and knees scrambled toward the wounded officer.

"What's happening out there?" Someone in the distance cried out.

"Call 911 and tell them we need the police and an ambulance." Davis' voice revealed the panic he was feeling. "Where are you hit?" Davis questioned his friend lying in the sand.

"It's my left leg just above the knee."

Davis removed his jacket applying pressure to Charley's wound. In minutes he could hear the sirens. The police were there quickly. Behind them came the medics. Charley was loaded into the ambulance. Davis climbed in with him. In the light Davis was able to see why his left rib cage had been burning. There was a hole in his shirt. Pulling the shirt up, Davis saw that the bullet had passed close enough to his body to leave a burn mark but had drawn no blood. At first he decided he was *lucky,* but then decided *blessed* was actually the more correct word.

At the emergency wing the young doctor on duty found that Charley's wound was not as serious as first thought, but he was admitted to the Falmouth Hospital. The slug had gone through his leg at an angle doing no damage to the bone. Davis spent the better part of the evening and early morning answering questions the Falmouth police were throwing at him. It was almost two a.m. before they were finished, satisfied that he and Charley had been targets of an unprovoked attack. Davis found Charley sound asleep in his hospital room deciding he would flop in the chair beside his friend's bed to finish the night. He had no desire to go back to the room alone.

The few hours spent in the chair could better be described as dozing than sleeping. Davis awoke stiff and tired when a nurse came into the room to check Charley's vitals and take a look at his wound. "You look like you need the bed more than I do." Charley's soft southern drawl was music to his ears.

"You gave me quite a scare out there on the beach. I thought he had gotten you."

"He came very close to getting both of us. I'm going to have to stop hanging with you. I'd never been a patient in a hospital in my life until I got tangled up with you. Now the count is up to two and probably climbing."

"There is no doubt in my mind that you saved my life last night. I'm grateful! I think I saw him when we were back at the motel in Boston. I guess I convinced myself it wasn't him. I should have told you. My foolishness could have gotten us killed."

"Don't worry about it! I was pretty sure he was there. That is why I went with you to the beach. I spotted someone showing a lot of interest in what we were doing shortly after getting to the motel in Boston. I didn't really need razor blades while you were napping. I was doing a little investigating while shopping. I decided there was no reason to alarm you unnecessarily, so I didn't say anything."

"We are going to have to stop keeping secrets from each other! By the way, where did you get a gun? I didn't think you were able to bring yours on the airplane?"

"Well...." Charley drawled. "You see, it wasn't a real gun. That is what I bought when I was supposed to be getting razor blades. I found a pretty real looking one in a Ben Franklin's toy department and bought it. I thought if he saw I was armed, he might not try anything. It almost worked!"

For once Davis was speechless! When his brain was finished pro-cessing what might have happened, he just shook his head in disbelief. "I thought those Falmouth police officers were having a little trouble getting their minds around my story. Do you think it might have had anything to do with the fact my police body guard was carrying a toy gun! I can hardly wait for them to talk to you. No one back home is going to believe you fought off our attacker with a phony gun."

"I would just as well not tell them." The young cop spoke sheepishly.

A doctor examined Charley's leg a few minutes later announcing he would dismiss him after a nurse dressed it. He was told he would need to be on crutches for a while. Two Falmouth policemen appeared as they were getting ready to exit the hospital room. Their questions kept the two exhausted Georgians there for almost another hour. After being excused by the officers they decided to drive back to Boston where they located a place to stay near the airport. "There is a nearby church that I have heard a lot of good things about. I think I am going to attend their eight thirty ser-vice in the morning. I know it is not easy for you to get around on those crutches, but perhaps you would like to go with me. We should have plenty of time before our flight leaves."

Charley hesitated but finally responded, "Since I am supposed to be your body guard I guess I need to tag along, but I don't have any church clothes with me," he offered.

"You won't need a tie and jacket for this one. Grace Chapel is a 'seeker sensitive' church where you will probably not find one person among their more than fifteen hundred attendees wearing a tie." Davis was pleased to be able to knock down Charley's excuse. Maybe attending such a church would be just the ticket to spark some spiritual curiosity in Charley's psyche. Several times throughout the night Davis left his bed going to the window where he peeped through the curtains to get a view of the parking lot, but he saw no sign of their stalker.

Arriving at Grace Chapel shortly before the praise service started, Davis observed that the building looked more like a theater than a church. It was equipped with an elaborate lighting system and projection which included large screens on both sides of the platform. Davis noticed that Charley seemed to get into the lively music which was led by a praise team that included three vocalists and a band featuring guitars, bass, drums and a key board. The sermon presented by the "thirty-something" open collared preacher was simple and effective. It was worth the trip for Davis to hear him make one statement, "Jesus does not love people because of what *they* are. He loves them because of what *He* is. God is *love*."

As they left the church parking lot to find a restaurant where they could have brunch before going to the airport, Davis was pleased to hear Charley remark, "That was all right. If I could find a church like that at home I might go more often."

It's a start, Davis told himself. *It's a start!*

On previous trips Davis had always hated leaving the Boston area. This time he was relieved to board the plane for home. Ever since the shooting, he had been expecting to find the "rat faced' man behind him. Three close calls were more than enough to make him paranoid. *The man must have super human powers, how did he know we were in Boston?* That question continued to haunt Davis all the way home as he considered every possible answer.

As he packed his bag, getting ready to check out of his Woods Hole motel, the middle aged man in the grey sports coat was thoroughly disgusted with himself. *There is no way I should have missed him. I was no farther than thirty or thirty-five feet away. I've never missed anything that close in my entire life, even in the darkness.* He wondered how Charley got the gun. It was no problem for him. He had friends in Boston. Obtaining a gun was easy, but that should not have been the case for the young cop. His thoughts caused him to remember that he would need to find somewhere to ditch the hand gun before boarding the plane to return to Georgia. That shouldn't be a problem with water in every direction. He knew the boss would not be happy to hear his report when he did return. Again he had failed to get the job done. That was not like him. Failure was not something to which he was accustomed. He considered himself among the best in his field. This business with Davis Morgan would not help his reputation. The right reputation was important when you made your living as a hit man.

It was Sunday afternoon. Deidre was feeling better, almost relieved. On Saturday evening when Amy was out with friends a strange fear, like none she had experienced before, swept over her. She could not get her mind off of Davis. She could not shake the feeling that he was in some kind of serious danger. She spent much of the evening in her bedroom praying for his and Charley's safety. That dark feeling had now passed. Davis and Charley were scheduled to return this evening. Her heart told her everything was now okay.

Chapter 18

Safely back home Davis called Helen Townsend first thing Monday morning. Helen, now well past her eightieth birthday, probably closer to ninety, was considered by most Adairsville residents to be the most reliable authority of the town's history. "Hello, Miss Helen. You may not remember me, but this is Davis Morgan. I'm Miss Elaine's boy."

"Yes, Davis, I remember you, I have been following your ministry. Somebody told me you quit the Lord and moved back to town."

"I haven't quit the Lord, Miss Helen, but I am no longer a preacher. There is something I need to talk with you about. Is there a time today that would be convenient for me to stop by your place?"

"I'll be here all day," the curious older lady told him. "You can come by any time you wish."

"I'll be there some time in the early afternoon," he told her. A visit with Miss Helen was something Davis both looked forward to while at the same time dreading. He knew her as a delightfully unique lady. Her knowledge of Adairsville's past was fascinating. On the other hand, he knew from the tone of her voice on the phone that she saw it as her mission to bring him back to the Lord. It should be an interesting visit since "Miss Helen" rarely let up when she was faced with a mission.

Having been gone several days, there was catch up work in his shop with which Davis busied herself. Books needed to be readied for the shelves. A few had to be packed for shipment. He went to the post office where he mailed his packages and checked his box for mail. Nothing but bills, he noted. On the way out he met Pastor John who welcomed him back home. Davis was glad for the opportunity to tell the preacher about Grace Chapel where he and Charley had visited. "You got Charley Nelson in church?" John questioned with a raised voice before mumbling something about a "miracle."

Dean complained to Davis about almost getting his little brother killed when he stopped by the Little Rock Café for the meat loaf special. "I never knew preachers could be so unpopular," Dean told Davis. "What have you been up to?"

"I wish I knew," Davis responded not really wanting to talk with his friend about his present troubles. He ate quickly before going by the barber shop for a hair cut. He then drove over to Maple Street where Miss Helen lived.

Not seeing a door bell, Davis knocked loudly on the door frame. He admired the big white clapboard house with a porch that stretched all the way across the front. Like most of the older places in town, there was more than one big water oak tree in the front yard. Davis knocked again, this time louder and longer than before. Miss Helen was widowed young and had never remarried. This was the old home place where she grew up and lived all of her life, but for the three or four years she lived with her husband. Miss Helen's dad ran a general store in the early part of the twentieth century. He was once the mayor of Adairsville. She was proud to have been among the socially elite in the little town during her early years. Talking about "the old families", the parties and social events the "young people" enjoyed in those bygone days was a favorite past time for Miss Helen. Her appearance at the door was a reminder to Davis of a slower and gentler way of life that he sometimes longed to experience, a time of which he had often heard his own mother speak when he was a boy with a mind full of questions.

"Miss Helen, it's good to see you. I'm Davis Morgan."

"I know who you are. You've put on a few pounds, but I'd recognize you anywhere. I was at your wedding you know, and I was there when they ordained you to preach."

Oh no, Davis thought, *you would think she would at least give me a moment to get reacquainted before starting in on me.*

" 'Called to preach,' they said. When you are called to preach, it's for life. Didn't they tell you that?"

"Yes, ma'am," Davis knew that to debate the issue with this dignified lady with the inflexible mindset would be a waste of his time. He had about as much chance of changing her mind as he did of moving Boyd Mountain. "May I come in to talk with you about something, Miss Helen?"

"Sure you can." She pointed toward a sofa. "You sit down over there. I'll get you some sweet tea," she told him.

Having eaten only minutes before, he didn't need the tea, and long ago he had given up sweet tea, choosing to drink it unsweetened. But Miss Helen didn't offer him sweet tea; she told him she would bring him some. He wasn't about to disappoint her. Looking around the room while she was in the kitchen Davis noticed that the big room was neatly arranged with a mixture of furniture that included some that had probably been in the room for over a hundred years mingled with some that had been added from time to time through the years. All the pictures on the walls were from a much earlier era. He guessed the two faces in the large oval frames were Miss Helen's mother and father. He decided the portrait on the wall in front of him had to be Miss Helen when she was in her late teens or early twenties, probably before she was married. Despite the ancient hairstyle and fashions she was an attractive lady. Davis guessed she had more than her share of suitors in those days.

"Can I get you anything else?" Miss Helen asked. She handed him a glass of iced tea along with a white cloth napkin.

"No, ma'am. This will be just fine."

"They tell me you have a bookstore in town. I have been meaning to take a look at it, but I don't get out nearly as much as I use to. You call it the Corra Harris Bookshop, I've heard. I met her you know. She was quite a lady. She was a Methodist preacher's wife."

"Miss Helen, I need your help." He jumped in knowing he needed to change the course of the conversation or he could expect another tongue lashing for leaving the ministry. "What can you tell me about Dixie Adair?"

"Why, I haven't heard anyone mention Dixie Adair in years." Her face revealed an almost trance like concentration as her mind, no doubt, went back many years to where it was prone to be more keen than in recalling more recent occurrences. "Dixie Adair," she repeated the name as if it was a key to unlocking memories that had been fastened up for years.

"Yes, ma'am, could you tell me about her?"

"As I recall I was just a girl when it happened. Some of the men in town found a baby, a little girl, buried in the Oothcolooga Cemetery. Not buried like people are usually buried, mind you. She was buried just a few inches below the ground on top of a fresh grave. I believe the undertaker was one of those who found her."

"Did she survive?"

"Oh yes, she lived. She was a healthy, blue eyed baby."

"Who put her in that cemetery? And why?"

"No one ever knew for sure, but there was talk that it was her own mother. They said the unmarried girl got in a family way somehow hiding it until the baby was born. She then left the baby in the cemetery so no one would ever know her secret."

"Who was the child's mother?"

"I don't know if anyone ever really knew the answer to that question."

"Do you remember what the people were saying? Surely there was a lot of speculation about the mother," Davis suggested.

"Speculation? I don't know about speculation, but there was a lot of gossip. I never paid much attention to gossip. You know what the Good Book says about that?"

"Yes, ma'am, I do. I remember preaching a few sermons on the subject." Davis mentally kicked himself for reminding her that he was a "backslidden preacher," but her mind was fixed in the past where she missed the cue. "But it would be very helpful to me if you could remember what they were saying."

"The talk was...," she paused again as if unsure about whether she should tell what she had heard. "Back then the word was that it was a preacher's daughter that gave birth to that little tot. That is why she hid her condition for all those months. It would have killed her pa if he had known."

"What was the preacher's daughter's name?"

"I don't know that, never did. Even back then we had several churches and almost all the preachers had big families. It seems to me that in those days preachers had bigger families than anybody else. Wonder why?"

That was a subject Davis did not want to pursue with Miss Helen. "So you don't have any idea who the mother of the little girl was?"

"No idea."

"What happened to the baby?"

"I believe little Dixie Adair went to live at the Methodist children's home down near Atlanta. I don't think anyone around here ever knew what happened to her after that."

"Did people ever talk about Dixie's father?"

"I don't remember ever hearing anything about him." Miss Helen quickly turned to another subject. "Are you aware that evangelist Sam Jones, of Cartersville, was once the superintendent of that children's home? Now there was a preacher that understood what it meant to be a servant of the Lord!"

Taking note of the direction of the conversation, Davis knew it was time for him to flee if he was to avoid still more of Miss Helen's righteous indignation over preachers who turn back before finishing their task. "Miss Helen, it has sure been good to see you again. You have been extremely helpful."

"Come back and see me again. You know the best shepherds are the ones that visit their flock."

"I'm well aware of that Miss Helen. I promise you I will come again. Thank you for your help and the tea."

Chuckling, Davis thought the Good book says, "*...his anger lasts only a moment...,*" (Psalm 30:5) *but I'm afraid Miss Helen's disapproval will last much longer.*

Pulling back the bulky drapes to watch through her living room window Miss Helen observed Elaine's boy as he walked off her porch and down the drive way to his car. *There goes a troubled young man*, she surmised. She recalled that it had only been a year or so since he lost his wife. *I don't know much that is harder than that!* It had been more than a half century since Alex, Miss Helen's own spouse, had gone to be with the Lord, but she still remembered well her grieving during those first months after his death. There were still times, after all these years, when she missed him terribly. She thought of him often when she sat down for dinner in the evenings. Sundays without him were still hard. *I don't know what else is troubling him, but I wish I could help turn the sadness I see in his eyes to joy,* she thought. After a moment she decided she could. Miss Helen sit down in her favorite chair, the one in which she was seated while Davis was with her. She began to pray:

"Lord, I understand that you know more about what is troubling that boy than I do. I get the feeling that he is desperately trying to stay afloat in some really deep water. Lord you need to throw him a life preserver because he is going to have a hard time making it on his own. He is a good boy. I know you can continue to use him in your service. Strengthen him and protect him. Lord you know that I did not intent to fib to him by not telling him everything I know. Sometimes not knowing is better than knowing. If you decide he needs that information, you can take care of that, but I will not be the one to let the cat out of the bag..."

After finishing her prayer Miss Helen continued to sit in her chair as her mind turned to earlier and more active times. After a few minutes she slipped into a light sleep until she awoke with a crick in her neck, no doubt, caused by her awkward position in her chair.

Visiting Miss Helen had whet Davis' appetite to visit with several other town characters that had been so much a part of his early life. He had seen very few of the old crowd from his mother's generation since being back in town. Many of them were now gone, but he thought of several who were still around, men and women for which he had real admiration. Most of his visiting had been done at the Little Rock or at the Post office. These people were no longer out and about as they had been in the years before he left town for college. He needed to make an effort to see them on their own turf. Davis decided that would be high on his agenda in the days ahead. He knew there was much to learn from such people.

Chapter 19

After visiting with Miss Helen, Davis decided to return home to catch up on some rather urgent house keeping chores that had piled up on him while he was in Boston. He began his work by putting clothes in the washer. While he was running the vacuum cleaner over the carpet in the living room the phone rang. He picked up the handset hearing the caller identify himself as Ralph. It took Davis a moment to realize that the "Ralph" who was on the phone was Ralph Hayes from the Crown Creek Church.

"Yes Ralph, it is good to hear from you. How are things at Crown Creek? We had a great time with you folks the Sunday we were there."

"That is why I called." The old timer spoke much louder into the phone than was necessary. "Me and Brother Frank are about to make a trip into town. We would like to stop by to talk with you if you are going to be around. It's about the church."

"Sure, I don't have any plans to go anywhere. I would be happy to have you fellows drop by. Do you guys know where I live?"

"I think so. You do live in your mother's house, don't you?

"That's right. It's the big house on Railroad Street in front of the school property."

"I know exactly where it is. We can be there in about half an hour if that is okay with you."

"That will work great. You guys be careful". Davis instructed his friend with a laugh, but he meant what he said. He had recently driven behind Ralph on south broad street. It was obvious the elderly gentleman's driving skills were deteriorating rapidly. During the five minutes it took Davis to finish vacuuming his living room carpet he pondered possible reasons Ralph and Frank would want to see him. He finally decided it must be the window he had broken escaping from "the rat faced" man and his partner. Perhaps they still had not been able to match the glass. Maybe it wasn't that at all, but rather repercussions to the sermon he preached there. He could not think of anything he said that day that could be considered controversial. Davis was extremely curious about the mission of the two Crown Creek elder statesmen to his home and just a little bit apprehensive.

There was just enough time to pick up around his living quarters and activate the coffee maker before the door bell rang. "Come in fellows. Find a seat." Not having any knowledge of why these gentlemen were calling on him Davis was trying his best to be warm and upbeat. He offered them coffee, but both men politely declined. Davis decided that was probably a wise decision on their part since his coffee was suspect at best.

Davis seated himself in a chair facing the sofa where the two white headed gentlemen both wearing overalls, were sitting. There was a short period of awkward silence before Davis again spoke. "It would please me very much if you gentlemen were here as my friends to simply visit, but I have a feeling that is not the case. Is there some way I can be of service to you?"

"Yes there is. You know we don't have a pastor at Crown Creek. Me and Brother Frank make up two thirds of the search committee. So far we have had very little luck in locating prospects. It seems to me that most of the younger men coming out of seminary want to go on staff at larger churches in larger cities or else be the pastor in no less than a county seat town. It is hard to find someone who is interested in a little country church like ours. Our people really enjoyed your message the Sunday you were with us. We came to ask you to consider becoming our pastor."

This was one possibility Davis had not considered when pondering possible motives for the surprise visit by the two gentlemen from Crown Creek. The request left him speechless. His guest no doubt noticed the shocked expression on his face. Frank who had said little up to this point jumped in speaking rapidly. "We need to move into the twenty-first century, and we believe you are the man who can take us there. Crown Creek doesn't have much of a future unless we start reaching some young families. Our resources are limited which means we cannot pay you the kind of money to which you are accustom, but we understand you have a bookshop. There would be no objections to you supplementing your church salary by continuing to operate your business."

Davis took a deep breath before responding to the two men sitting on his sofa anxiously looking his way. He spoke softly and perhaps a bit slower than usual. "I want you gentlemen to know that I am humbled and deeply honored that you would want me to be your pastor, but there are a number of reasons why it is just not possible. The fact is I left my church in Indianapolis because I felt I could no longer do the job. The time may come when that will change. Circumstances may be different someday. The Lord may or may not lead me back in that direction, but right now I need a breather in the worst way."

It was Ralph who offered the rebuttal. "It is different at Crown Creek. If I understand it correctly your church in Indiana was a large church with several hundred members while we are a smaller church. Why, it would be hard to find thirty families who attend three Sundays a month. I am sure we would require far less energy than what your last church demanded."

Davis knew he would not be able to explain to the men in his living room that his decision had little to do with the amount of work required. "Don't fool yourself Ralph. There is just as much work for a preacher to do in a small church as a large one, perhaps more. Reaching and discipling people requires much effort regardless of the size of a church. In a large congregation the pastor usually has a number of specialists on his staff allowing him to basically teach and supervise; however, in a smaller body the pastor may have to wear many hats. Another reason I am probably not the best man for you is that I have no experience serving rural churches. Your people might be better served by having someone who knows the in and outs of rural ministry. You mentioned the need to reach young families. That is certainly true, but I am well past being a young man. The young families in your community would probably respond much better to a younger pastor."

"Oh, you are still young', Frank responded with a laugh. "Most of the people at Crown Creek are our age, a few are even older. I am sure there are many pros and cons, but the bottom line is our people want you to be our preacher. We have prayed about it and the good Lord doesn't seem to have any objections. Maybe you could spend some time talking with Him about it."

"I promise you I will do that, but I don't want to give you any false hope. As things stand now I do not believe the Lord is leading me to Crown Creek or to the pastorate of any other church. I am flattered that you gentlemen as well as others in the congregation would want me, but I do not feel it is the direction in which I am being led at the present time. I am thinking of two or three people that might consider taking the Crown Creek pastorate. They are good men that would do a fine job. Why don't you let me give you their names, addresses and phone numbers?"

"We would rather have you," Ralph responded, "But, if we can't convince you, we would very much like to have those names and numbers."

Davis got off of his chair strolling to a small table that had been his mother's pride and joy. He pulled an address book out of the drawer along with a pad of paper and a pen proceeding to write three names and phone numbers on the top sheet before walking it over to where the men were seated and handing the sheet to Ralph.

Ralph, handling the piece of paper as if it were pure gold, carefully folded it placing it in his shirt pocket under the bib of his overalls. The men talked for a while longer before starting to make their way to the front door. As Frank was walking through the door to the porch he turned suggesting to Davis, "Let us know if you change your mind".

"I will be sure to do that, but please don't count on me changing my mind any time soon. You contact those men whose names are on that piece of paper I gave you and you will probably find your preacher." After the two men left, Davis sat down in his recliner for a few minutes to ponder what had just happened in his living room. Ten or twelve years ago after spending time with a friend who had just written a book about knowing God's will, Davis had completely changed his position on that subject. Prior to that time he had always felt that God had a plan as to where and when he wanted us to serve. It was up to us to pray and seek God's will in order to determine where God wanted us at any given time; however, Davis never had a clear understanding about how we could expect God to show us His pre-determined direction. He had the notion that the Father used various methods of getting His will across to us. We just need to keep our hearts and minds open. Somehow He will show us what he wants us to do.

Under his friend's influence Davis changed his position coming to believe that God wasn't so concerned with where and how we served him as long as we were doing so in some fashion. That which matters, he decided, is that we stay within the boundaries of God's instructions as found in the Bible. His friend called it the *big umbrella*. It really doesn't matter where we are located while we are doing that. It was with that philosophy that Davis had made the decision to leave Indianapolis and come back to Georgia. He sometimes wondered if perhaps he was simply using his friend's theology to justify doing what he wanted to do. Maybe God did want him at Crown Creek or as pastor of a church somewhere else. Perhaps God had intended for him to stay in Indiana. How could he be sure he was in God's will? Finding the answer to that question was extremely important to the former pastor.

After turning it over in his mind for a while Davis decided that coming to definite conclusions about such matters in the midst of all that was going on in his life right now was rather difficult. He had often counseled people not to make major decisions in times of crisis unless it was absolutely necessary and only then with great caution. He would be able to think more clearly when "the rat faced" man and his partner were taken off the street and his life settled into a more normal routine. Davis got out of his chair returning to the task he had started before getting the phone call from Crown Creek. He felt a little like he had supposed a man in a science fiction novel he had once read felt; a man caught between two world's not sure which world to embrace. He decided that when things settled a bit he would talk with Pastor John. It would be interesting to know the young preacher's thoughts about finding God's will for one's life.

The two men from Ohio sitting in the front seat of the white mid size car parked on the north end of town in the parking lot beside the Methodist Church annex building carefully watched the old blue truck move from Morgan's driveway where it slowly went south on railroad street. "Well, there goes the truck," the man in the tan shirt on the passenger side addressed his friend sitting behind the steering wheel.

"Yes, but that police car is going nowhere."

"Why should that hinder us? That is just a hick cop and no more than a kid at that. It would be easy enough to take him out."

"Yeah, I am sure we would have no trouble taking care of him, but the surest way to start an all out man hunt is to bring down a cop. The law doesn't look kindly on the killing of their officers. I would just as well stay away from that unless I get a chance at that kid that is always hanging with Morgan."

"What's our next move then?"

"Let's get the girl. They are not watching her very closely. There will be plenty of opportunities to grab her. If we continue to keep our eyes open the chance to get Morgan will also come, and I can hardly wait. Usually those who I am hired to take care of are just marks. I have no feelings about them one way or another, but I am looking forward to bringing Morgan down. I've been looking forward to it every since he sprayed that stuff in my eyes. Did you hear what the boss said he was calling me? His name for me is 'the rat faced' man. He is not so pretty himself. I'll show him who the rat is!"

"I don't think the boss was happy about the money spent on your trip to Boston without getting any results. The tab is getting rather steep. You know how the boss is about spending money."

"I wasn't real happy about the lack of results myself. I have put down some real men in my time, and I did it without any difficulty, on the first try. I don't know why it has been so hard to get this wimp! He is nothing more than a pansy book selling preacher."

"Maybe that is the problem. Perhaps he is getting help from the man upstairs."

"I don't care who is helping him. Pretty soon he is going to be a dead man. You can count on that. I have completed every single contract I have ever been given. This one will be no exception. I will get it done."

"Don't you think we had better be moving on? I am afraid if we sit here too long we will draw some attention from the cops."

"These dumb cops have a hard time finding their way home. They are not going to give us any real trouble, but you are right. We probably should not stay in one place too long." "The rat faced" man turned the ignition key starting the engine. They drove through the square turning west at the end of the street onto Hotel Street.

Chapter 20

When Amy arrived home from school she took a telephone call from her dad. "For several weeks now you ladies have been feeding me every Monday night. I think it's my turn. Dinner is on me tonight."

"That sounds great! What are you cooking?" Amy asked.

"Well, I thought we would go to the Inn. The food will be better there than if I prepare it."

"And besides…," his daughter knowing him well said, "You don't have to wash dishes at the Inn."

"Not unless I run short of money."

"You know, I really do need to spend the evening in the library. The paper I have to do for the class I'm taking toward my Masters is due next week. Why don't you and Deidre go and I'll take a rain check. She needs to be at the high school auditorium by seven for the chorus' end of the term concert, but you two could have an early dinner. Maybe you could go with her to the program. She hates going to those things alone."

"It's okay with me if it is acceptable to her."

"I am sure she will be delighted. You could pick her up around five o'clock. That would give you plenty of time for dinner."

"That will be perfect. Tell her I will see her at five."

Amy had not lied to her father. She did need to finish the paper, but she had to admit to herself that the arrangements she had just made were concocted primarily to get her dad and Deidre together alone for the evening. She had simply taken advantage of a situation that had fallen into her lap. Amy knew Deidre would probably have her hide if she knew what she was up to. Her roommate had never actually told her she had any romantic interest in her dad, but now that Amy had started watching and listening a little closer, it seemed obvious that there was potential for something more than casual friendship.

If anything was to come of their relationship, she would need to help it along, Amy decided. It was true that her dad was spending a lot of time with Tracie, but perhaps that was because Tracie was "safe." Her Father knew that nothing serious could ever come of their courtship. *Getting over the feeling that he would be betraying Mom would be the bigger obstacle,* Amy thought. *...And I am sure he is very much aware of the age difference between him and Deidre.* Deidre was another matter, having been hurt severely once she was not about to put herself in a position for that to happen again. She was probably also sensitive to the fact that he was her roommate's dad. *Yes,* Amy decided. *I have my work cut out for me if I am going to succeed as a match maker.*

In the past couple of weeks Amy had given it a lot of thought deciding it would be a great match. Deidre was just what her dad needed and he was exactly right for Deidre. The more she thought about it, the more she was convinced she was not wrong. It was true that she could never think of Deidre as "Mom". She was too close to Amy's own age. Deidre had already become her big sister, but to see two people she loved so much together would be a dream come true. *Age is just numbers,* she decided. Many couples with a lot of years between them have found happiness. *Maybe nothing will come of it,* she thought. *But if it doesn't it won't be because I didn't give it a shot. It's not like I am trying to create something from nothing. There is definitely affection between the two of them.*

After getting off the phone Davis began to feel as if maybe he had been set up, but he really did not mind. He looked forward to spending an evening in the company of the attractive young woman who showed up so often in his thoughts.

Nothing was learned from Davis' call to the Methodist Children's home in Decatur to inquire about Dixie Adair. Even if he had been able to talk someone there into giving him information, it would have done him no good since there were no records available for the period prior to 1935. It seems there had been a fire or some such disaster which had destroyed all the records. Evidently Mr. Brown suspected that Dixie Adair was the second child Judson Reed fathered during his stay in Adairsville. The time sequence would be about right. It would explain, at least in part, the Dixie

Adair mystery. But it still did not offer an explanation for Ed Hagan's murder, nor did it present any clues to the attempts on his own life. Perhaps what Ed had wanted to show him had something to do with Dixie Adair, but why would he want to show it to him?

Since the rumor involved a preacher's daughter, Davis decided it might be helpful to gather whatever information could be found about the pastors in town during the years from 1925 to 1930 along with their families. That would not be an easy task to complete. The only way Davis knew to get the job done was to contact each church office, or in the case of the smaller ones, someone prominent in those congregations who would have access to records. One after the other he made the calls finding almost everyone cooperative, but, in most cases, unable to immediately give him the information for which he was asking. They each agreed to do the required research getting back to him as soon as possible. He contacted the three Baptist churches that would have been in existence during those years, the two Methodist churches, the Christian Church, and the Cumberland Presbyterian Church located several miles from town. His contact with the Church of God revealed it, like some of the Baptist churches out in the rural areas of the county and the Church of Christ, had not been organized until more recent years. He looked down the listings under Churches in the yellow pages to make sure he had covered them all.

By the time Davis finished with the calls, it was time for him to meet Deidre for dinner. They waited only a few moments for a table since it was early. Few people had yet arrived. He ordered a steak, she chicken. "Have you ever been to New England?" Davis questioned his dinner companion remembering his thoughts on the beach just before the ordeal with the "rat faced man."

"No, I haven't. Actually, I have traveled very little outside of Georgia. When I was a child we did not take family vacations. Of course, like everyone who lived in South Georgia, I've been to Florida often. While in college I visited in the homes of friends in Tennessee and South Carolina, and I have visited relatives in Alabama a number of times. I flew to Cincinnati once for a seminar and once to Lexington for the same reason, but that is about the extent of my travels."

"Being a history teacher, you would love New England. Julie and I always appreciated Cape Cod. It was our special vacation spot," Davis said reflectively.

140

"You still miss her a lot don't you?"

"You don't know how much! You can't be with someone for all those years and then suddenly give them up without feeling that you have lost a part of yourself. I still find myself turning to ask her a question when I am home alone. Sometimes in the morning before I get up, forgetting that she is no longer with me, I hear noises that I automatically assume are her stirring around as she always did in the morning. She was a morning person. In so many ways we were different. I think that is why we were so important to one another. We compensated for each others' weaknesses. As individuals, we were average, but together we made a pretty decent person. I think I understand why the Bible speaks of husband and wife becoming one."

"I would like to have known her. She had to be special to rear a daughter like Amy and to have impacted a person's life as much as she has yours."

"I wish you had known her. You would have loved her, and she would have loved you. In many ways the two of you are alike. Your simple business like approach to everyday living, your natural sweetness, your way of sort of blending into the background, but yet making your presence very much known, always concerned more about the other person than yourself."

"I don't know that I have ever received a compliment I appreciate more. I am glad you feel that way, but I hope I'll never disappoint you. You've put a lot of pressure on me you know."

"There is no pressure. All you have to do is just continue to be yourself."

"Is Amy a lot like Julie?"

"In some ways she is. How could she not be? For all those years Julie nurtured her, loved her, and was her constant companion. They were as close as any mother and daughter I have ever known. She could not help but take on many of her mother's attributes. She walks like her, she talks like her, and her laugh is a carbon copy of Julie's. More importantly she embraces the same values; however, Amy's personality is her own. She is much more aggressive and outspoken than her mother. Amy is the type of person ready to take life head on. Julie would rather sneak up on it. But sometimes I feel Amy is the only reason I've been able to bear the loss of her mother. She is the part of Julie to which I still have access."

"I suppose that is why you have had such a hard time accepting her marriage to Jay?"

"It shows, huh?" Davis was a little disappointed that Deidre had picked up on his attitude toward his future son-in-law.

"A little, but I think you are making good progress."

"Yeah, I think I am, but I still have a ways to go. I know I am still the doting father, but I'm working on it."

"Have you talked with Tracie since getting back to town?"

Deidre's mentioning of Tracie threw Davis a little off balance. It wasn't that he did not want to talk about her. He was shocked to realize he had actually forgotten about her momentarily. "I've tried to call her a couple of times, but I've only gotten her service. I suspect she is out of town. She doesn't sit still for very long, and she has the means to come and go as she pleases. Is there any particular reason you ask?"

"No, I just wondered how your relationship with her is developing. It appears you are rather fond of her."

Deidre's candor made Davis a little uneasy. "I do like her a lot. I enjoy being with her. She is fun. I think being around her causes me to feel young again. That may be because we spend so much time reliving our high school days. We had high school crushes on each other back then, but never did anything about it."

"And you accuse me of being the ladies' man." A male voice that Davis immediately recognized came from behind him.

Without turning to look, Davis said, "Hi, Charley. How is the leg?"

Charley hobbled on his crutches to Davis' side. "Better watch out for this guy," he told Deidre. "He'll get you killed. There are people all over the country taking shots at him. I hope you have on your bullet proof vest."

"Nothing can happen here with the crack Adairsville police department on the job. I suppose I got you a leave of absence. It must be nice not having to get up and go to work in the mornings."

"What you got me is a place behind a desk for several weeks. I'm not even allowed in a patrol car."

"What more could you want?" Davis asked. "A nice, safe position with absolutely no risk, no school crossings, and no traffic patrol; and still drawing the big money."

"Yeah, it's great," he added sarcastically. "I'm making so much money I may be forced to actually open a bank account. I'd better get back over to Gail," he said pointing to an attractive brunette who smiled and waved when they all looked her way. "You had better think twice before agreeing to go out of town with this guy," he suggested to Deidre. "You could end up on crutches or worse."

"Take care, Charley. Don't work too hard."

"He is cute," Deidre giggled as Charley returned to his table.

"I'm not sure *cute* is how I would describe him," Davis replied trying not to show his displeasure over Deidre's obvious attraction to his young friend.

"I hope not," she laughed.

Charley's a little younger than Deidre, he reasoned, *but he's a lot closer to her age than I am*. That thought dampened his spirits a bit.

"He reminds me of the boys in my classes," she offered.

His mood suddenly transformed Davis felt compelled to defend Charley. "He has a lot of growing up to do, but he is a good man. I am alive today only because he knows his job. He is a good cop."

"Well, I'm glad for that. I would sure hate not having you around," she said with a smile.

It was past six-thirty by the time they finished their meals. Davis paid the tab before driving to the high school. Adairsville is fortunate to have one of the finest new high school facilities in North Georgia, but Davis missed the old location behind his own house. He was rather surprised at the high quality of the musical presentation by the high school group. Davis tried to stay focused on the program, but found that difficult with the affect Deidre's perfume along with the warmth of the touch of her shoulder against his was having on him. Such reactions still caused him to feel guilty, but no matter how hard he tried he found it very difficult to subdue his feelings toward this fascinating young woman. He took note that he was now thinking of her as a woman rather than a girl. He was not sure he approved of that shift in his thinking.

Davis was sorry to see his time with Deidre come to an end. It was fun, but he would now go home alone spending the evening watching what was left of the Braves' game. He continued to feel guilty about enjoying her company as they went their separate ways on the front porch. He tried to evaluate his feelings. Did he feel he was betraying Julie or Tracie? Maybe it was the age difference or the fact that she was his daughter's friend. For whatever reason, he couldn't get away from the feeling that enjoying her company so much was somehow inappropriate. He heard Amy enter her apartment a few minutes after he got home, and he breathed a little easier knowing she was safe next door.

"How was dinner?" Amy questioned her roommate with a smile on her face.

"It couldn't have been better. Did you get a lot of work done at the library?"

"I've finished most of my research. I just need to sit down at the computer and give it some kind of form. The real work is finished."

Deidre considered lecturing Amy about her match making, but decided not to bring it up. Perhaps it had been completely innocent. She would give her friend the benefit of the doubt. Besides it had been a great evening. She hoped there would be more time with Davis in the days to come, but she wondered if she had a right to wish for such a thing. As much as she tried to stifle it, she could not help being attracted to the older man who happened to be the father of her best friend. She wasn't sure if that was appropriate, and she wasn't sure if Davis felt the same way about her. She knew he liked her and even respected her, but sometimes she feared he saw her only as an immature girl, his daughter's friend. And, of course, there was the thing with Tracie. Perhaps if she got up enough nerve she would make an appointment with Pastor John to seek his counsel. At this point she was not sure she wanted to do that.

Chapter 21

It was much later in the week before Davis got the information he had requested from all the Adairsville churches. At first glance there didn't seem to be anything that would help him get a handle on what was going on. The only name on the various lists of preacher's families he recognized was one he previously knew would be on the list. His own mother's foster mother, the lady he considered his maternal grandmother, Mary, was a preacher's daughter. Her father served churches in North Georgia all his adult life. Most of those years were spent in Bartow County. That was not new information for Davis. He would see what he could find out about these ministerial families, but he was disappointed that nothing on the various sheets of paper he had accumulated jumped out at him. He wondered why he expected it to be so easy. There had been nothing simple about this thing from the beginning.

He continued to call Tracie. After a time she returned his calls from Cincinnati. "I still have business interests here", she explained to Davis. "There are some details I couldn't put off any longer. It will be a few days yet before I can return. I would much rather be there with you. It is awful hard being in the big city knowing I could be enjoying the clean air of North Georgia. I sure miss you. I hate not being near you. I hope you haven't found someone else since I have been away."

Feeling a little uncomfortable upon hearing that last statement Davis was quick to respond. "I'll be right here when you return," he assured her. "It is not like beautiful ladies are lining up to compete for my attention. I am fortunate that one has decided to keep company with me. I certainly don't intend to do anything to jeopardize my relationship with her. I don't think you have to worry about me finding someone else."

Tracie asked about the welfare of Amy and Deidre before terminating the call with the words, "I love you".

On Thursday morning, Davis scheduled to go to Rome to keep a speaking engagement with a community organization was strongly urged by the police chief to remain in Adairsville where they could keep an eye on him, but by now he was becoming a little stir crazy. When he insisted on keeping the engagement, the chief suggested he take Charley along in an unofficial capacity. Charley was glad to get away from his desk, but was somewhat disappointed when he learned that it was a senior citizens group they would be visiting. Not a good place for Charley to meet young ladies.

"Is this something new?" Charley asked him on their way to Rome. "Do you speak to these groups often?"

"It's something I did from time to time when I was in the ministry, but what I'm doing today, and I hope often in the future, is a little different. I am talking to them about collecting books by Georgia authors."

"That should be exciting," Charley sarcastically replied. "I think it might be more interesting to hear you preach, and you know how much I like preaching."

Yes, I know, but I am praying that will change. "You listen closely today and you might learn something."

"What is there to know about Georgia writers? Margaret Mitchell wrote *Gone with the Wind*. That is all there is to know."

"Your education has been sadly neglected. Do you know what Georgia author won the Pulitzer Prize for fiction in 1934?"

"That would probably be Margaret Mitchell for *Gone With the Wind*.

"That wasn't until three years later. In 1934 it was won by a young woman still in her twenties who married her high school English teacher. The prize winning title was *Lamb in His Bosom*. The author's name was Caroline Miller. She continued to write up to the day she died, not too many years ago, but only one other of her books attained any success. It was called *Lebanon*. Published ten years after her first novel it made much less of a splash than the earlier work. I'm told she left bundles of unpublished manuscripts when she died. You need to come by the shop and buy a copy of *Lamb in His Bosom*. It's a good read." Davis continued, "Did you ever hear of an author by the name of Will Harben?"

"No, can't say that I have."

"He was a prolific writer originally from just up the road in Dalton. He wrote more than thirty books in a thirty year span from the late eighteen hundreds into the early twentieth century. W.H. Howell, the well known writer and critic, considered him one of the best writers of his day. He defended Harben to Mark Twain who evidently didn't think highly of his skills. Most of his stories were about the hill people around Dalton. It's sad that he has almost been forgotten even in his home town. A few years ago when we were in Georgia on vacation, I took Amy with me to Dalton to try to find his old home place. Almost no one we talked with had ever heard of him. It took a while to discover that his home place had been torn down about three years prior to our search. We did find his grave, however. He was one of the finest writers of his day. I still get his books from time to time. His first was based on a true story about a woman who lived in Dalton spending the first part of her life as a white slave. Then there was the post Civil War humorist known as Bill Arp. His real name was Charles Smith, a gentleman farmer-lawyer who lived first in Rome and later in Cartersville."

"Enough already," Charley put his hands over his ears. "I don't want to listen to your speech twice."

"Oh, the material I'll share with the group will be different than what I've just told you. It saddens me that so many people in Georgia have so little knowledge of our literary heritage. I want to do my part to change that."

"Besides, if you can get them interested, you can sell them some books."

"You've got it! You keep hanging around with me, and you may end up in the book business yet."

"I can't see that happening, but if you get rich I might give it a try."

"People don't normally get rich in this business, but I'm convinced the go-getter with a good knowledge of his craft can make a good living. I'm staking my future on that belief."

"I hope it goes well for you, but we have got to keep you alive for that to happen. Keeping you alive seems to be getting more and more complicated."

They arrived at the Senior Citizens Center in time to eat lunch with the group that had gathered, after which Davis gave his talk. He spoke of Carson McCullers, Flannery O'Connor, Lillian Smith and some contemporary Georgia writers such as Anne Rivers Siddons and Terry Kay. He spent some time telling the cordial group about the late Eugenia Price who had come to St. Simons Island, Georgia to live after spending time there researching her first inspirational novel, *The Beloved Invader*. His presentation was well received triggering a number of questions during the question and answer time. Only Charley seemed to be bored.

On the way home, they talked about Dixie Adair, Mr. Brown, Judson Reed, the "rat faced" man, and Ed Hagan coming to no new conclusions. "By the way," Charley interjected, "We learned that Ed Hagan rented a safety deposit box at the bank just a few days before he was killed. The teller told us he used the bank's copier, kept the copies he made, putting the originals in the box. It is probably nothing, but we will have the proper authorization to check it out in the next day or two."

"Maybe it will be the lead that will enable you to solve this case. It doesn't seem like you've gotten many breaks up to this point."

"Good police work is about seventy-five per cent perspiration. You keep plugging away, and, sooner or later, you get what you need."

"That sounds a lot like the ministry, the book business, and just about every other type of endeavor. Keep on keeping on is some of the best advice I ever received. Will you let me know if you come up with anything in the safety deposit box?"

"Sure, and you let me know If you uncover anything with this Dixie Adair thing. Even if it has nothing to do with the case, I'm curious." The two retuned to Adairsville mid-afternoon. Charley was dropped off at the police station while Davis returned to his shop where he mostly chatted with Janie and several browsers until closing time.

On Thursday at noon time Davis with his newspaper in hand walked from his shop down the street to the Pizza Palace where a lunch buffet was served each day. He put three slices of pepperoni on his plate carrying it to the table in the corner along with a small salad and a diet coke. As he was reading his paper while eating he heard someone call his name. Looking up he saw Sam Ellison, the mayor, standing beside him with a tray of food.

"May I join you?" The mayor looking dapper in white shirt and black bow tie was addressing him. "I have wanted to talk with you for a while," the seventy something, bald headed gentleman told Davis as he was already seating himself.

"Sure Mr. Mayor, I would be delighted to have such distinguished company. A good meal is always made better by good company."

As he took his food and drink off the tray placing it at the end of the table, the mayor told his table partner, "A group of us were talking about you the other day."

Davis laughed. "I hope the conversation was positive."

"Oh, it was. We were talking about how talented you are."

"I'm glad someone has decided I have some talent. I've never thought of myself as being particular gifted in anything other than the ability to persevere. Tell me, what is this talent that your group has discovered I have?"

"We hear you are a good writer. Someone told me you have written a book as well as a lot of articles. They also tell me that you are going to be a regular contributor to our newspaper."

"Yes, that is all true, but I don't know that I am a gifted writer. I enjoy writing, and by preparing sermons for years, I have learned to organize my material."

"That is good because someone needs to write a history of our town. It has never been done. We believe now is the time and we believe you can do it. I told the committee that whoever writes this history needs to do it while Miss Helen is still around, and sharp enough to remember all that she knows."

"You are right about that. Miss Helen would be the best source of information, but I am not sure I am the person to do it. There must be someone in town that is more qualified than I."

"I don't know who it would be. We couldn't think of anyone else with any writing experience. There is that Johnson girl who has written two or three romances, but she moved out of state more than three years ago."

"I'll give it some thought and let you know what I decide in three or four weeks."

"That would be good. We have several of the civic groups lined up to pay for the printing. We think it will not take long till there will be enough sales to reimburse them. After that anything that comes in is your."

Sure, Davis thought, *the writer will likely never see a cent; however, it is a worthy project that I would like to see completed.* While he knew it would be yet another big commitment of his time with very little return, it was a worthy project that interested him.

As Davis and the mayor continued their meals the conversation turned to the Ed Hagan murder. "By the way, Sam, do you know anything about the Dixie Adair affair?"

"I've heard the story. I think it happened way back in 1929, but I don't really know anything about it. That was before my family moved to Adairsville."

"Really? I thought your family had probably been here for generations. I know you have been around for as long as I can remember."

"My family moved here from Mason, Ohio when I was seven years old."

"Mason, isn't that near Cincinnati?"

"Yes, Mason is a suburb just north of that city."

"I need to get back to work Mr. Mayor. I'll let you know about that town history in a few weeks."

The next few days went by without incident. Davis used the time to prepare for the big festival and the thousands of potential customers it brought each year. It would be his biggest three business days of the year and it was just days away. He would need to be ready if he was to reach his potential for sells. He gave himself to his work, but the "rat faced" man was always in the back of his mind. The bookseller was never completely comfortable. That would only happen after the feared villain was no longer a threat. Davis hoped that would be soon.

Chapter 22

———✦✕✦———

Amy had always enjoyed a good party. Davis wasn't sure where that came from since he avoided them like the plague. Julie had enjoyed entertaining a family or two at a time, but like him she was not high on parties. Previously Amy had told him that Deidre's birthday was coming up. She wasn't sure what they would do, but she wanted to recognize the occasion in some way. Her plans started as a get together with a few friends, but when Amy learned that Deidre's childhood included no birthday party of her own, it evolved into a full fledged surprise party involving mostly people from school and church.

The community club house, just a couple of blocks down the street from their Railroad street residence, was secured for the occasion. The quaint brick club house known as the Sans Souci club was named for the women's club that had met there for many years. The original group had raised the funds to build the building more than seventy-five years previously. During Davis' childhood it doubled as a library. Amy and two of her school teacher friends decorated the building, bought a huge cake along with other refreshments while concocting a story about a meeting that would enable them to get the honoree there without giving away the actual reason for all the cars in the parking lot when they arrived.

When Davis got there along with Charley who was in uniform the party was already in progress. Davis carried a dozen red roses he had picked up from the florist just before closing time. He waited several minutes for Deidre to get free so he could present them to her. Finally when he saw an opportunity to jump in, he quickly approached her, handing the roses to her with the words, "Happy birthday sweet lady." He pulled her toward him giving her a gentle hug while kissing her on the forehead.

The birthday girl flashed him that beautiful smile he had come to treasure in recent weeks. "The roses are beautiful. They are my favorite."

"A little birdie told me that," Davis laughed

Let's get a vase from the kitchen so we can put them on the table with the cake," Deidre suggested. They walked together toward the kitchen. Deidre with roses in hand, looked up at Davis remarking, "I thought you weren't coming. I would have been greatly disappointed had my best friend not shown up."

Davis did not let the remark about being her best friend get past him. "I would not miss it for the world. If anyone deserves a special night, it is you."

"I don't know about that, but it sure was nice of Amy to do all this work for me. This is my first birthday party, you know."

"I know that, but I am sure there will be others in the future."

"I think any future parties would be anticlimactic. One great party like this should suffice for a lifetime."

After the roses were placed in the middle of the table someone called out, "It's time for cake." Deidre was pulled toward the table while the candles were being lit by a young teacher that Davis recognized as Kevin Adams. Someone started to sing happy birthday. Soon everyone joined in as Deidre stood in front of the cake with that beautiful smile on her face. After the singing subsided, Deidre was instructed to make a wish. She looked in Davis' direction before closing her eyes and then blowing out all twenty-nine candles.

Davis stood away from where most of the guests were assembled looking around him at those in the room as the cake was being cut. He spotted Jerry Evans, the high school principle and his wife, Lori, who might be three or four years older than him; otherwise he could find no one in his age bracket. That distressed him a bit.

Walking over to where Davis was standing alone Charley asked, "Why the sour look? There is plenty of food, and pretty girls are everywhere you look. How could anyone be unhappy with that combination?"

"Oh, I'm not unhappy Charley, just in deep thought. I have a lot on my mind. Isn't Deidre beautiful tonight? When Amy started planning this whole thing I was a little concerned. I was afraid Deidre would be turned off by such a big to do, but obviously she is enjoying herself immensely, as one ought to enjoy her first birthday party. I'm glad! She deserves it. She has had a rather rough life, but she sure has come out on top. Deidre is a remarkable woman."

Charley looked at the expression on Davis' face as his friend focused on Deidre who was laughing as she was conversing with Kevin Adams on the other side of the room. Charley remarked to his friend, "Boy, you have got it bad don't you?"

"Oh no, it's not like that!" Davis responded rather unconvincingly. "I admire her greatly. She is a special person, one of my very best friends, but there isn't anything romantic about our relationship."

"I'm sure of that," Charley laughed. "I can tell by the way you are looking at her that there couldn't possibly be anything romantic between the two of you."

"I'm almost old enough to be her father," Davis remarked for his own benefit as much as for Charley's. "She could never be romantically interested in an old man like me."

"You sell yourself short Davis. How old are you anyway? Maybe forty-five or forty-six? That is not old. You are probably the youngest forty-five year old I know."

"I appreciate you saying that, but the fact is I am still seventeen years older than Deidre. When she is my age I will be sixty-two years old. When she is sixty-two I will be seventy-nine."

"So what? That's no big deal. If you love her you should let her decide if age makes any difference."

"I didn't say I love her. I said I respect her greatly. I said she is one of my best friends."

"Spending all those years in the pastorate you should know a lot more than I do about real love, but isn't that what love is? Isn't love respect, affection and friendship?

Davis was caught by surprise with his young policeman friend's insight. "You make a good point Charley. Maybe you ought to be the pastor."

"That would shock a lot of people I know," the policeman laughed. Let me warn you Mr. Bookseller. If you don't snatch up that girl, I'm going to go after her myself, and when I go after a girl I generally get her. You are right! She is beautiful all the time, but she is radiant tonight."

Charley walked away keeping his eyes on the activity in the little club house. Davis knew his friend was enjoying the party, but he was there to do a job. Charley could be counted on to do that job well.

After another hour or so the crowd began to thin out. Davis was tired, a condition tied to his age, he reasoned, but he had promised Amy that he would stick around to help clean up. In a few minutes only he, Deidre, Amy, Charley and two other young female teachers remained. The group refused to allow the birthday girl to participate in cleanup. Charley was not quick to get involved. That left Davis, Amy and the other two ladies, so it took awhile to put things back in order. Before leaving the little club house the group of six sat down around a table for a little conversation and rest before heading home.

"This is just about the nicest thing anyone has ever done for me", Deidre told her companions. "This evening will always have a special place in my heart. Thank you for being my friends." As she spoke Deidre reached for Davis' hand gripping it tightly at first, then allowing her smaller hand to lie in his big left hand. They sat there that way for a few minutes. Davis hated to get up when it was time to go, but he knew it was necessary.

The hour was late when Amy and Deidre finally got back to their apartment. Deidre hugged her roommate, thanking her for her thoughtfulness as well as her hard work on her behalf. Before going back to her room shutting the door behind her Deidre remarked to Amy, "Everyone should have a friend like you."

Amy's guess was that Jay had already turned in for the evening, but she just had to call to tell him about Deidre's evening. When Jay answered the phone with a "hello" that did not sound like him at all, Amy knew she had indeed awakened him. When she apologized Jay responded, "Haven't I told you again and again to call me day or night regardless of the time? How did the party go?" Jay knew his fiancée well enough to know why she had called at such a late hour. She was not able to keep her excitement all bottled up.

"It was marvelous! Deidre was either totally surprised or else she is the best actress in the world. There was a great turn out. I think everyone we invited was there as well as two or three we didn't invite."

"Did the birthday girl enjoy herself?

"I don't think I have ever seen her have so much fun. It seems to me she has finally turned the corner on the *Jeff ordeal*. On our way home tonight she told me that until recently she had considered Adairsville just a two or three year stop over until she decided where home would be.

She said that has now changed. According to her Adairsville is home. It is where she wants to spend the rest of her life."

"I feel sort of that way myself." Jay was finally able to get a word in edge wise. "I've been thinking, instead of scanning ads for an apartment; why not line up some houses for us to look at when I return. Since I want to make Adairsville my permanent home, and I know that has always been your desire, I think it would be wise for us to go ahead and buy a house. If we combine the money I have saved with the stock my dad left me, we should have enough down payment money to keep the monthly payment manageable."

Amy was thrilled! It was exactly what she had dreamed of, but had not wanted to push Jay into a situation with which he would be unhappy. It was well past one o'clock before they got off the phone. It was after two-thirty before the hyped up Amy could get to sleep

Chapter 23

John was not usually in his office late afternoons. From the beginning of his pastorate which was just four years earlier when he received his Master of Divinity degree from the Cincinnati Bible Seminary, the plan had been to use mornings for office work such as study, administration and counseling. Afternoons were for visitation and making his presence in the community known. If he had learned anything in his short ministry it was that a preacher could not count on staying with a schedule. It was almost four o'clock and here he was waiting for a counselee to arrive. Deidre Ross called the previous day asking to see him at around four o'clock. He had agreed even though it went contrary to his plans. While he sat at his desk wondering what she needed from him, Louise, the church secretary, knocked on his office door announcing; "Pastor, Deidre is here."

"Send her in." The young preacher stood moving from behind the desk to greet his counselee who he calculated to be about his own age.

"Come in Deidre." John met the attractive school teacher at the door greeting her with a warm smile and a hand shake before pointing her toward a chair in front of his desk. He seated himself in the other chair just a few feet away from the one in which Deidre was seated. John had learned that he communicated better when he did not have a desk between him and the person with whom he was visiting.

Noticing that Deidre seemed a little ill at ease John began the conversation by trying to tell the young woman how much he had appreciated having her in his congregation over the past months. "Your presence has been a real blessing to us. I am glad for the opportunity to get to know you a little better. It's hard to build a relationship with people when you only see them in a pew while you are preaching. Thank you for coming by. Is there something I can help you with?"

There was a moment of silence as Deidre obviously collected her thoughts. "Actually, I guess there are a couple of things about which I need to talk with you." She turned her head toward the preacher making eye contact. "First, let me say that I have appreciated your sermons. They have helped me deal with some of the irritations that have been a part of my life over the past months, and I have learned a bundle from you. And the people have been wonderful. They have accepted me, giving me a family here at the other end of the state from where I grew up. It looks like Adairsville is going to be home for me indefinitely. I would very much like to make this my official church home. I know I have been attending for nine months now. This is something I should have done six months ago, but I guess better late than never."

"I'm pleased you want to make it official even though we have thought of you as part of our family for some time. I assume you are a baptized believer. Perhaps I should not assume anything. Let me ask, are you a baptized believer?"

Deidre quickly answered the preacher's question. "Oh yes," she emphatically replied.

"Then all you need to do in order to become a part of the church here is to walk forward at decision time when I will introduce you to the congregation as one who has chosen to be part of the body in this place. We try to keep it as simple as possible."

"That sounds easy enough, even for someone as shy me.'

"We couldn't be happier to have you. I am sure someone as gifted as you will add greatly to our ability to minister in this community."

"There is one other thing with which I could use some help. I don't really know where to start," she said looking down at the floor. "This is sort of hard for me. When I try to put it into words it sounds rather silly."

The pastor spoke encouragingly. "I have learned that when there is something on my mind it is best just to speak up."

"I'll do my best, but before I say more I need to know that everything I tell you will be held in complete confidentiality. Can I count on that?"

"Absolutely," the pastor assured her. "Whatever you tell me will be left in this office."

"I think you know that just before I came to town I had planned to be married. Well, I won't go into detail, but everything fell apart just a couple of weeks before the wedding was scheduled. It was cancelled. I was convinced that any possibility of my ever being a wife and mother had come to an end. At that point I am not sure I wanted to consider marriage again. I know now that was just a reaction to the hurt I was experiencing at the time. The bottom line is there is now someone for whom I have strong feelings. I am not sure if I am in love with him. While I know he likes me a lot I am not absolutely sure he has any real interest in me romantically. I just need to know that if something should come of our relationship, it will be appropriate? Would such a relationship be Biblical? Would it be practical? There was no one else for me to come to but you."

The young preacher looked a little bewildered. "I didn't know you were seeing anyone."

"I'm not exactly seeing anyone," Deidre answered.

"I need to tell you that when it comes to matters of the heart I am not an expert. I am not yet four years into my own marriage. When it comes to romance I am still sometimes in the dark; however, as your friend and pastor I will certainly advise you if it is possible for me to do so. Why do you question whether a relationship with this person would be appropriate? Is he a Christian?"

"Oh yes, I don't think I have ever known a more devout one. Perhaps the main reason I question the appropriateness or perhaps a better word is "wisdom" of such a relationship is the difference in our ages. He is seventeen or eighteen years older than me."

"I am sure you realize there is nothing in the Bible that would forbid a relationship between two people with such an age gap, but there are certainly some practical considerations. I'm guessing the person we are talking about is now in his mid forties. Should the relationship progress and ultimately lead to marriage will he want children? You need to ask yourself, can I live with his decision should he not want them? Our interests seem to fluctuate at different age levels. Will your interest remain sufficiently uniform with this age gap? Then there is the problem of health. We don't know what the future holds, but the odds are great that he will begin to experience health failure that comes with age well before you. It very well could become a nursing situation for you. Would you be able to handle that? I have known a few people, such as a couple in my home church, who have made it work with more years than we are talking about between them. I have also known those who failed because they did not give due consideration to these factors."

"I have given a lot of thought to each of those questions. As to the matter of children, Yes, I very much would like to someday be a mother; however, I think if I should marry a man who did not want children and I knew that going into the marriage; I could live with his decision if ours was a strong loving relationship. I am sure you are right that our interest may vary some at different age levels, but don't you think it is possible for two people, especially two Christians, to have basically the same focus for their entire lives toward the things that really matter? The health issue could be a consideration regardless of our ages going into marriage. I believe two people entering marriage must make a commitment to do for one another whatever the situation dictates."

"It sounds to me like you are giving adequate thought to the possible problems that come with age differences. That is good. Are there other concerns?"

"Yes, there are. For one thing he is a widower. His first marriage was special. He loved his wife very much. I don't know if anyone will, in his eyes, ever measure up to his deceased wife. I think his lingering love for her is one of the things that drew me to him, but at the same time it scares me away. I'll never be all that she was, and I know that. I don't know if he can live with anything less."

"You are wise to be concerned about that. It is true that can be a problem; on the other hand, it is certainly possible for a man with such a capacity to love to continue to love his deceased wife for whom she was, while loving you for who you are. The question then is does he really love me? If the answer is 'yes' you have nothing to fear."

"Theoretically I agree, but I am still sorting through this one. I guess I'm just not yet convinced. Perhaps if or when I know he loves me it will be different. There is one other concern. It happens that he is my room-mate's father."

The last statement caused John's mouth to drop open. He suddenly realized they were talking about his friend Davis and that shocked him a bit. He wasn't sure he liked the position that put him in.

Deidre continued to speak. "I value our friendship greatly. She is like a little sister to me. I don't want to do anything that would threaten our relationship. Sometimes I think she knows how I feel about her dad and is even pushing the relationship, but I wonder if I were actually there in the place her mother had once occupied if she would feel the same way."

"I guess you realize you have just identified for me the person about whom we have been talking?"

"I realize that, but there is no reason to keep that a secret from you since you have assured me that this is all confidential."

"I guess not. Let me just say that Davis is one of the finest people I have ever known. There is no one this side of Heaven to which I look up to more. I think I can assure you that should he make a commitment to you, it would be the real thing. I don't believe there is anything phony about him. Should the time come when he would again take a bride he will love her with all of his heart for a life time."

"That is exactly the way I see it, but I think I needed to hear it from someone else."

"As to Amy's reaction to any relationship with her father, you can expect her to respect whatever direction her dad takes. I am sure it will not always be easy for her, but she loves her dad. She wants what's best for him. She will trust his decisions."

The two, pastor and soon to be church member, talked a while longer about matters of the heart as well as church life before Deidre got up to leave.

"I do appreciate you talking with me. You have helped me immensely. Please remember that any relationship between me and Davis is in the beginning stages. Perhaps not even that. Under the circumstances I just needed to bounce the whole thing off someone. I certainly don't know what to expect down the road. Nothing may come of it."

"I'll be praying about it. In fact, I would like for us to take it to the Lord now." John took Deidre's hand praying with her for the Lord's guidance in her life in the days ahead. Afterwards they chatted for a moment longer before Deidre left through the door through which she had arrived.

After Deidre had left his office, John continued to sit in the chair in front of his desk in deep thought. After four or five minutes Louise, who had been instructed to remain in the building as long as Deidre was there knocked on his door announcing, "I'm on my way out. Is there anything you need before I leave?"

"No, I can think of nothing, you enjoy your evening and I will see you tomorrow morning." John continued to allow his mind to dwell on what Deidre had told him. In a thousand years he would not have guessed that anything was developing between Davis and the young teacher. He had seen them together a great deal, especially at church. Then why, he asked himself, did it so surprised him? He decided that it must be because of the age difference. The more he thought about it though the more sense it made. They are both quality people each going through a time of extreme loneliness. They are exactly the kind of people who would be drawn to each other. *I certainly believe Deidre would be better for him than the widow he has been seeing recently,* he decided.

As much as the young preacher admired Davis, his friend had become somewhat of an enigma to him. Why would a successful pastor leave a flourishing church in a city like Indianapolis to come back to Adairsville to open a bookshop, of all things? John loved the people in his church. The work was for the most part satisfying, but he would give his right arm to have an opportunity like the one Davis had willingly given up. John knew that a certain amount of ambition was a good thing, but he was aware that too much could become a problem. He would need to keep his guard up. Davis was capable of managing his own life he decided. He locked the door of his office and headed for his car. He had not seen Heather, his wife, and their seven month old baby boy since leaving home early this morning. There were visits which could only be made in the evening on his *to do* list, but he decided he would spend the evening at home. Those visits could wait to another day. His family needed some attention from him as well.

Amy was not home when Deidre returned to her apartment. She was glad to have the time to herself. Pastor John had told her nothing she did not already know, but it was good to have what she thought she knew confirmed. This whole thing frightened the living daylights out of her. Her instincts told her that Davis was gradually becoming more and more attracted to her and that scared her. Sometimes she felt that he was just being his gracious self having no real feelings for her and that scared her even more. She felt as if she could not possibly again endure the kind of hurt that had so gripped her a year ago when she and Jeff had ended their relationship. Would she be setting herself up for that to happen again should she be responsive to Davis? Life is much more complicated than it should be she decided.

In the midst of her thoughts Deidre's phone rang. She picked up the handset putting it to her ear sweetly speaking into it, "Hello".

She heard the voice of Kevin Adams, the fellow teacher with whom she had gone out a few times. "Deidre this is Kevin. It has been a while since I've had the opportunity to spend any real time with you. Being with you at the party reminded me of how much I've missed you. I thought I would check to see if perhaps you would like to go with me to Kennesaw tomorrow evening for dinner and a movie."

"I do appreciate your invitation Kevin. It is nice of you to ask me, but I think I had better stay around here. I do have a good deal to do. I probably would not be very good company."

The two teachers talked of work and mutual friends for four or five minutes before politely ending the conversation.

Well, that's that, Deidre decided. *That ends any future relationship with Mr. Adams.* Deidre wondered, *have I set my sights too high.* She reasoned; *Kevin is a decent person. He is rather handsome with a good personality. Most girls would be glad for an opportunity to go out with him. Why can't I be happy with someone like him?* After giving that question careful consideration, Deidre decided it was his lack of maturity with which she had a problem.

When Deidre sat down to read she caught herself listening for Davis' car. She didn't necessarily need to be with him, but she did need for him to be safely in place next door. Between ten thirty and eleven o'clock she heard his car pull into the drive. After a few moments his footsteps could be clearly heard as he walked across the porch. Then she heard the sound of the door closing next door after he had gone inside. No more than ten minutes later she was peacefully sound asleep beneath the covers on her bed.

Turning lights on in front of him as he walked to his kitchen to get a glass of orange juice before he went to bed, Davis was reminded how much he despised coming home to an empty apartment. He remembered how neat it was to know that regardless of what time he got home Julie would be there when he arrived. Even when he got home extremely late she would usually be awake waiting for him. She had told him more than once that it was difficult for her to sleep until she knew he was safely home. It was special to have someone who cared so much. It was nice to have someone to come home to.

Chapter 24

———◆✕◆———

"The Great Locomotive Chase Festival" is Adairsville's signature annual event. During the Civil War a Union officer by the name of James J. Andrews, along with several soldiers, captured a train, the General, north of Atlanta. The plan was to destroy the tracks and bridges behind them all the way to Chattanooga. They were chased by Confederates on board the Texas. The chase passed right through Adairsville. The story has been told in several books and in a Disney movie produced in the nineteen fifties.

Twenty-five years ago, someone with a mind for promotion came up with the idea of a festival with "the great locomotive chase" as the theme. It caught on. One weekend late each spring is packed with events starting with a parade on Friday morning, a beauty pageant, square dancing, concerts, mock gun fights, street dances, fire works, and more. All traffic is rerouted around the downtown area where booths are set up along the streets with vendors selling crafts, food, and novelties. Carnival rides are put in place for the children. The events are near the old depot that sits beside the still active tracks. Trains creep through the festivities. More than one hundred fifty thousand people usually walk through the streets of the quaint village during festival weekend.

The early June weather was perfect for this one. It had been promoted well through newspapers and radio in the surrounding cities. The 1902 Stock Exchange would open early and close late throughout the weekend. Davis planned to be in his shop most of the three days. He had stocked the shelves with several 1936 copies of *Gone With The Wind*. There were only five thousand copies in the first printing in May of that year, but before the year ended nearly two million came off the presses. They could still be bought. He could sell them at a good price in Georgia, especially at an event such as this one. He had located a number of books by Corra Harris. They were of little value in other parts of the country, but brought him a good profit in the Corra Harris Bookshop. Davis had even been fortunate enough to come up with two copies of *Andrews Raiders*, a book about the Great Locomotive Chase. It should be a profitable weekend for sure, he decided.

Chief Hanson stopped by his shop on Friday morning. "You understand that with all the congestion, we will have a hard time keeping tabs on you the next few days," he told Davis. "You had better be careful. Keep your guard up and your head down." The warning was not taken lightly. Davis knew the "rat faced" man and his partner would have a better chance of getting to him with all the strangers in town than any time since the ordeal started. He would be on guard, but he would not let it spoil his weekend. He planned to enjoy all the excitement. Having lived away from Adairsville all those years, he had not attended the festival since one of the very early ones when it was a much smaller event.

After the ten a.m. parade, a large crowd gathered upstairs in the theater for a presentation by an Abe Lincoln impersonator. The guy was good, but Davis decided the audience in this case would have enjoyed Robert E. Lee or Jeff Davis much more. He looked over the crowd casually. He doubted the "rat faced man" or his partner went in for cultural events. All morning and afternoon people wandered through his shop. He sold several books, mostly Georgia material and children's collectibles. Nancy Drew and the Hardy Boys were doing well. He enjoyed meeting and talking with a number of people from out of town He especially liked visiting with local residents he had not had contact with for years, some of them having been high school teammates and classmates.

Amy and Deidre showed up in the late afternoon. "We came to take you to dinner," Amy declared.

"That's great," Davis told her. "Being seen with two beautiful and charming young ladies should enhance my reputation."

"We live to serve," Amy responded. "What will it be? Maybe Georgia barbeque or Polish sausage? Or maybe you would like to go down to the fish fry," she joked knowing he did not care much for fresh water fish.

"Let's see if we can find some barbeque and a table where we can sit down and eat," he suggested. "I have never liked eating while trying to balance my food at the same time."

They found a place behind the business section near the carnival rides where a local civic organization had set up a tent like the ones used at grave sites. As a matter of fact, it had the name of the town funeral home on the flap that hung from the top. Picnic tables had been set up under the shelter. Deidre quickly perched in one of the seats at the one empty table before other customers could get to it while Amy and Davis went to secure the food. The meat was being barbequed on site in a contraption that looked like it had been constructed out of scrap metal. The vendor also sold Brunswick stew which Davis could never turn down. Brunswick stew was one of the things he missed most when he lived in Indiana. He ordered a pork barbeque sandwich and a coke to go with his stew. Amy ordered beef barbeque for herself and Deidre along with fries. Davis had always felt that beef barbeque wasn't barbeque at all. It had to be pork to be the real thing.

"This looks good," Davis declared putting the food on the table as he climbed over the bench portion of the picnic table. "The problem I have finding good southern barbeque is that the health department has closed down all the good places," he laughed.

"That tells me something about your eating habits," his daughter responded.

"Well, how has business been today?" Deidre asked.

"It has been excellent. Much of what I have sold has been of local interest, but you expect that to be the case with the customers you get through an event such as this one. They aren't necessarily book lovers, but many of them are interested in local history."

"Do you have any thing in stock about Pretty Boy Floyd?" Amy asked.

"No, several books have been written about him in recent years as well as in the past, and I have had some of them in stock recently, but they are all gone."

"Why would Pretty Boy Floyd be of special interest to local people?" Deidre inquired with a puzzled look.

"Don't you know about the Pretty Boy Floyd-Adairsville connection?" Amy asked surprised that anyone could live in Adairsville for almost a year without hearing the stories of Charley Floyd playing at the depot as a boy. "You do know who Pretty Boy Floyd was I assume?"

"Of course, I do. Remember I am a history teacher, and while depression outlaws cannot be classified as major American history, they are a part of our American lore. But I was under the impression he lived in Oklahoma or somewhere in the West."

"His family moved out West when he was ten or twelve years of age. He was born about five miles east of here in the Folsom community. His family moved him into town when he was a toddler. They lived in that house over there." Davis pointed to a house just across the railroad tracks. "Adairsville residents are not going to let the world forget that the infamous bank robber's roots are in this little North Georgia town."

"I'm not sure it is such a good thing to draw too much attention to us," Amy suggested. "If too many people discover our town, we would loose some of our uniqueness. I think one of the charms of our community is that it is a sleepy, laid back village that has not changed as rapidly as some others."

"I do not disagree," Deidre responded. "I would not want it to change drastically; however, a community that does not accept some change will soon find itself in a sorry state."

"You are right," Davis agreed. "But I believe Adairsville's future could very well be in its past."

"What do you mean by that?" Amy asked.

"Look at that," Davis said pointing to the strip of buildings known by local residents as the downtown business district. "How often do you see a town that still looks pretty much the way it looked a hundred years ago? Visualize all of those buildings restored as the Stock Exchange has been: the drug store with the lunch counter and soda fountain, and that big building in the middle of the block that once was a general store as another major antique outlet. The Depot would be a great museum and the old cotton gin over there," Davis pointed in the opposite direction. "It could be restored and opened to the public. How many of us have ever seen how an old fashioned cotton gin operated? You can see several warehouses from here that would make great antique malls, and the people would come. I'm convinced they would come with the proper promotion. We just need a few more citizens with vision."

"Seems like you have it all laid out," Amy concluded. "All we need is a few million dollars and we are on our way."

"Who knows," Davis spoke softly almost as if he were talking to himself. "Maybe we'll have it some day."

"Are you going to escort us to the concert?" Amy asked. "I hear the band they have tonight is an 'oldies band.' That should be right up your ally," she added.

"Depends on how old their oldies are." Davis really didn't want to be reminded that he had a good number of years on both the young ladies sitting at the table. "It is still over an hour before the concert starts. Let me go back to the shop. Hopefully I can make a few more sells before then. I'll meet you in front of the depot when it's time. In the meantime you ladies can look at the crafts or whatever."

"That sounds just right. Come on, Deidre. I saw some beautiful quilted bags down at the other end of the street." Amy spoke while picking up the empty paper plates and cups pitching them into the big trash container.

Davis made his way back to the Stock Exchange passing the checkout counter where Janie, who by this time looked a bit frazzled, was checking out a long line of customers. "Looks like you need some help," he said as he went by.

"I wish you would tell the boss that," she shot back.

There were several people browsing in his shop when he arrived. "Do you have anything on the Great Locomotive Chase?" one of the customers asked immediately.

"I just happen to have the best work on the subject right here," he said pulling one of the books out of the local interest section.

Staying busy helping customers Davis found that the time to meet Amy and Deidre came quickly. They were in front of the Depot waiting for him when he arrived. The band wasn't the best he had heard, but he did enjoy their selection of tunes from the sixties. Amy and Deidre seemed to have a good time, but he was sure he enjoyed the show much more than they did.

Davis was dead tired when he finally crawled into bed after midnight. He slept soundly rising early the next morning to the buzzing sound of the clock next to his bed.

He skipped breakfast, but prepared the coffee maker. After shaving, showering, and dressing he went out to get the Saturday paper. To his delight he found it on the porch. Sometimes neighborhood dogs beat him to it. He paused on the porch for a moment to enjoy the morning sounds. He looked across the road and tracks where he could see the Inn surrounded by big water oaks. South of there was the business district. A few people were already stirring about getting their booths ready for the onslaught of prospective customers that would start in a couple of hours. He could hear a dog barking in the distance. Not the high-pitched bark of a small breed, but the deep course bark of a real dog. The sound of an automobile could be heard only occasionally.

The festival is a good thing, especially for those of us who have retail businesses in town, he decided, but he loved Adairsville best when it was just Adairsville, his Norman Rockwell village. He longed for things to get back to normal. Oh, the festival would be over late Sunday, but the normal he longed for was the one that could only come when the "rat faced man," his partner, and whoever was behind the horrendous things that had so upset his world were somehow eliminated. His return to his hometown, so far, had not been what he expected. *But then, is anything ever what we expect?* He took his paper inside sitting down with it and a cup of coffee at the kitchen table.

The constant flow of friends and strangers who came into his shop throughout the day was enjoyable for Davis. They often came in groups of three and four. The majority of them only browsed. Some asked for that which he did not have in stock. More often than not they asked for tales they remembered reading as children, sometimes having no idea who the author was. Davis was again reminded how limited his knowledge of literature really was. At times he thought of himself as an authority, but then three or four consecutive customers would ask for books and authors he had never heard of. It could be humbling.

Amy was about as happy as a young woman could be. She was glad she had made arrangements for the fitting today. It got her away from the festival congestion. She had fun seeing herself in the big mirrors all dressed up in her wedding grown with the long train. It was times like this that she missed her mother most. *Mom would have loved being part of all this*, she told herself. She had hoped Deidre would make the sixty mile round trip with her, but she did not push when her roommate was reluctant. She understood why she would find such activity difficult. She didn't want to complicate her roommate's life. Amy had made out fine on her own.

With preparing and grading final exams along with all the other busyness necessary for closing out the school year, Amy had thought very little about her upcoming wedding over the past few weeks. Now that school was out she intended to enjoy everything about the process. There were still a lot of last minute plans to make and implement, but time was not a problem for her now that there were no classes to prepare, nor teach for at least ten weeks. As she drove, Amy took a CD from its case putting it into the player. There was music to select for the pre-ceremony program. This CD, which she had just purchased at the bridal shop, would help her make those decisions. She wished Jay could be with her in the coming weeks. Doing all the planning and preparation long distance was not the best way, but they would manage.

She was glad that her dad had finally started to warm toward her fiancé. His attitude had bothered her for a time, but it didn't take her long to realize that it wasn't that her dad had anything particular against Jay. At this point he probably would not have been ready to give her hand to anyone, but she knew that he loved her. She had always known he would come around in time. He would trust her to choose that person that would make her happy. *Dad knows what it is like to love someone with all his heart, and to be the recipient of such love. I know Jay and I can have the same kind of happiness I saw in Mom and Dad during their years together.* She had been thrilled last week when her dad asked to speak to Jay during her nightly conversation with him. He had talked for almost twenty minutes. *Dad rarely talks on the phone for twenty minutes to anyone,* A good sign she decided.

Amy's thoughts were interrupted by the automobile on her bumper. Noticing there was a passing lane at this juncture in the road, she slowed down hoping he would go by her. Instead the driver pulled beside her swerving in her direction. She steered left and slammed on her breaks. The driver pulled in front of her when she came to a halt. Almost before she could comprehend what was happening a man jumped out of the passenger side of the other car. He was standing beside her with a gun pointed in her direction. When she saw the twisted smile on his face, she knew immediately who he was. He looked exactly as her dad had described him. It was the "rat faced" man. Her heart almost stopped with the fear that overcame her.

Charley came into the shop. "I'll be with you in a moment," Davis called out while trying to help a customer decide on which Chip Hilton story he would purchase for his son. Davis suspected the customer was more interested in the sports stories than was the boy. "You don't find these in this kind of condition with such perfect dust jackets very often," he told the father.

"I understand that, but the price seems a little steep."

"They are not inexpensive books. They are very collectible. You would have to pay thirty-five to fifty percent more in Atlanta."

The man selected two of the titles, both baseball stories. "You can pay the lady at the check-out desk near the door." Davis pointed him toward Janie.

"What can I do for you?" Davis turned toward Charley. "Have you finally decided to take up reading?"

"It will be a cold day in July when I start buying your high priced books. The chief sent me over with this," Charley took a folded sheet of paper out of his back pocket handing it to Davis. "This is a copy of what we found in Ed's safety deposit box," he explained.

Unfolding the paper Davis silently read. "Wow!" he exclaimed after a couple of minutes. "This is a shocker."

"I suspect this is what Ed wanted to show you the night he was killed."

"He probably found it in my attic or somewhere in my house while he was there working."

"The bad guys probably didn't know he had put it in the safety deposit box. I figure he was going to show you the duplicate he had made at the bank," Charley added. "I suspect they found the copy, but realizing it was not the original, they destroyed the house to make sure it would never be found."

"I suppose Ed had earlier approached whoever stood to inherit the remainder of the Reed fortune with this in an effort to extract some of the money for his own pockets?"

"That is my guess. It was probably his greed that got him killed. The heir, whoever he is, probably refused to give in to Ed's blackmail. Then, true to his threats, he was going to show it to you when that person's hired killer put a gun to his head just before you arrived."

"But how did Ed know about the Reed fortune? And how did he find the heir when we haven't been able to do so?"

170

"Men like Ed have a way of finding anything that will pad their pocketbooks. If I was you, I would be calling our lawyer friend at Cape Cod," suggested Charley.

"Do you think this will be enough to get him to tell us who Reed's known heir is?"

"I don't know. This doesn't prove anything," Charley said pointing to the paper in Davis' hand, but it sure pulls the whole thing together. We may not be able to prove it, but we know why they are after you."

"Can I keep this?" Davis asked holding up the sheet of paper.

"Sure that is the copy the chief made for you. Keep your eyes open." Charley offered the warning as he was making his way through a group of people.

For the next couple of hours Davis moved among his potential customers almost in a daze, unable to get his mind off the letter he had folded and placed in his shirt pocket. He decided he should share the contents with Amy as soon as possible. He picked up his cell phone punching Amy's number, but it was Deidre who answered.

"Deidre, this is Davis. Is Amy home?"

"No, she drove to Rome for a wedding gown fitting. She left her cell in the charger. She should be back anytime."

"I've told her time after time not to leave the house without her cell. Would you have her call me as soon as she returns? It's really important!"

"I'll tell her."

"Thank you."

The next two hours passed quickly with potential customers in the shop at almost all times. The sun was getting low in the sky, still Amy had not called. Maybe Deidre forgot to give her the message. He called Amy's cell again. Again Deidre answered.

"Amy's still not home?" Davis questioned.

"Not yet. I'm beginning to get a little worried that she may have had car trouble or something. I know she planned to be home in time for us to drive to Calhoun for dinner."

It wasn't mechanical problems that concerned Davis. The contents of the letter Charley had brought him earlier made it clear that her life could be in as much jeopardy as his.

"Do you know the name of the store where she bought her gown?'

"Yes, it was Henderson's Bridal Service, but I am sure they closed at five or six."

"Let me know immediately if you receive any news." By the time another hour passed with Davis hearing nothing from Amy, he knew something was wrong. He would walk home, get his car, and drive the route to Rome, hopefully finding her. He couldn't stand around waiting while his little girl might be in trouble. As he was leaving the Stock Exchange, he saw Chief Hanson and another officer coming toward him.

"Wait up, Davis," the Chief called out. Davis could tell by the grim expression on his face when he got near that Chief Hanson was the bearer of bad news.

"What is it, Chief?" he anxiously inquired.

"Davis, there has been a bad accident."

Davis' heart was sinking. "It's Amy, isn't it?"

Chapter 25

———✦✕✦———

"I'm afraid you're right," Chief Hanson told Davis. "It is Amy. Before you jump to any conclusions, let me tell you that she is still alive."

The information did little to console Davis. He could tell by the tone of the chief's voice that it was serious. "What happened," he asked.

"We don't really know. The accident was over on the Snow Springs Road. Several people who were in the yard across the road from where it happened said Amy came over the hill and around the curve pretty fast. She ran off the road rolling the car into a tree. The man sitting in the passenger side did not have on a seat belt. He died immediately. I've got to be honest with you, Davis. Your daughter has some head injuries. It doesn't look good. They probably have her at the hospital by now."

"Which hospital?"

"Floyd County Medical Center in Rome."

"Who was the person with her?" Davis asked already moving down the street toward home where his car was parked.

"We don't know. He was so banged up that no one at the scene could identify him. He had three pieces of I.D in his wallet all with different names and information. There is one more thing you might like to know. We found a gun at the scene. I don't suppose Amy owned a gun, did she?" The chief asked as he walked rapidly trying to keep up with Davis who was continuing to move toward home.

"No, definitely not. She inherited her mother's fear of guns. She wouldn't get near one. I'll talk with you later Chief. I've got to get to Amy." Davis was almost running now.

When he got to the house Davis hurried toward the girls' door calling for Deidre. She met him on the porch, a look of dismay on her face. "Has something happened to Amy?"

173

"Yes, she is at Floyd County Hospital." They both walked rapidly toward Davis' car.

The trip to the hospital is usually at least a twenty-five minute drive. They made it in well under twenty with Davis trying to tell Deidre what he knew as he drove.

They quickly walked toward the emergency wing after Davis parked the car on the parking deck. "We are looking for Amy Morgan". Davis spoke to the woman behind the desk in a tone that made it sound more like a command than a statement.

"The doctors are with Miss Morgan now. Are you family?"

"Yes, I'm her father."

"Wait over there". The woman pointed to seats in a corner of the big room. "Someone will be out to talk with you shortly." When they were seated, Davis noticed for the first time Deidre's swollen eyes. He put his right arm around her shoulder and pulled her to him. They both broke into tears as he held her.

"I should have gone with her," Deidre sobbed. "If I had not been wallowing in self-pity, I would have been with her."

"There is no reason to think that you being with her would have changed anything except maybe both of you would be back there." Davis pointed in the direction where he assumed the medical personnel were attending to Amy. "I couldn't bear to loose both of you."

"What happened, Davis? This makes absolutely no sense. Why was she on an isolated road like Snow Springs? Who was the man in the car with her? Amy is one of the most cautious drivers I have ever ridden with. How could this happen?"

"I don't know. The important thing right now is her condition. Let's take it one step at a time."

Within ten minutes from the time they were seated, a middle aged lady wearing a white jacket came through the door that Davis surmised was the entrance to where emergency patients were being attended. She approached them. "Mr. Morgan? I'm Dr. Hearn," she said extending her hand to him.

Davis stood, taking her hand anxiously he asked, "How is Amy?"

"We are still trying to determine the extent of her injuries. She took a pretty good blow to the head. We can take care of the cuts and abrasions, but we have got to find out what internal injuries we are dealing with.

She is unconscious. It could be anything from a mild concussion to very serious injuries. At this point we just don't know. As soon as the radiology people finish, we will let you go back to be with her. Don't be alarmed by her appearance. The swelling will subside and the cuts will heal."

"Thank you, Doctor. I appreciate what you are doing for my daughter. We'll be right here when you are ready for us."

The lady in the white jacket left them walking at a pace that indicated the urgency of reaching her next destination.

"We had better call Jay," Davis turned toward Deidre. "Would you mind doing that? I think I have his cell number in my wallet."

"I'll take care of it. I'll step outside."

Deidre returned after about five minutes. "He will be here as soon as he can get a flight out. We will not have to meet him at the airport. He said he would rent a car."

"Good. Thank you for handling that."

The result of receiving Deidre's call was pure panic for Jay. How could he even think well enough to make the arrangements to get to his beloved Amy? He took out his cell making reservations with the airline, but it would be several hours till his flight would leave. He called his boss, who did not seem pleased that Jay would be taking emergency time for the next few days. Jay didn't much care what his boss thought. His place was with Amy. Next he packed a few clothes not sure if he had gotten what he would need. He sat for a while, but got antsy so he headed for the airport where he parked his car, making his way into the terminal to wait for his flight to board.

His thoughts were of the good times he and Amy had enjoyed together: the concerts they had attended, the many times they had laughed together often without provocation. He remembered the football games they went to as students and the times afterward when they, not having a lot of money to spend, would go to the hot dog joint for dinner. The long walks on the beach while holding hands was also a special memory for Jay. Most of his life had been a dull and serious affair. Most of the really fun times he could remember had been with Amy. Why would anyone want to hurt her?

Deidre had led him to believe that Amy's injuries could be serious. What would he do if anything happened to her? He didn't even want to consider such a possibility. All his plans and dreams included her. Life without her would be no life at all. The flight from Orlando to Atlanta was less than a two hour trip, but to the distraught young man it seemed like they would never arrive. Finally the plane was on the ground. Having taken his luggage on board, he was able to by-pass luggage pick-up going directly to the car rental desk, but he was directed to three different agencies before finding an available car. Now he was on his way, he could be with Amy in two hours or less!

After waiting an hour or so, which seemed much longer to Davis who kept looking at his watch, a nurse came out to lead them back to the cubical where Amy was lying on a gurney. Davis was glad the doctor had prepared them for her appearance. Even with that warning, he was shocked. He took her hand which seemed cold to him. During the forty-five minutes before they moved her to intensive care, she showed no signs of consciousness. Dr. Hearn appeared just before they moved Amy. "Can you tell us anything yet, Doctor?" Davis asked.

"We haven't found anything. It may be internal swelling that is keeping her in the coma, but at this point we just don't know." Davis and Deidre walked to the family waiting room near intensive care to wait out the night. They would not be allowed to see Amy until morning, when there would be a thirty minute visiting period for families of ICU patients, but they felt compelled to remain nearby.

After a while a tall man in a uniform appeared first talking to the woman behind the information desk. Davis saw her motion toward him before the man in blue uniform walked over to him. Davis recognizes his uniform as a Georgia State Police uniform. "Mr. Morgan, I am Ray Tidwell from the state patrol". He extended his hand to Davis as he spoke. "I am sorry about your daughter's accident. I hate to bother you, but we thought you might be able to help us. If you are up to it, we would like for you to see if you can identify the man who was in the accident with your daughter. He is in the morgue here in the hospital. It should take only a few minutes."

Reluctantly leaving Deidre in the waiting room alone, Davis left with the patrolman. They took the elevator down to the lowest level where they walked through a long corridor. Finally they entered a large room that looked almost exactly the way morgues are always staged in the TV dramas. When the body was rolled out and sheet was pulled back the cut and battered face of the man was in view, Davis had no trouble recognizing him. He was not surprised at his identity. It was "the rat faced" man's partner. Davis, in his present mental state, was a little disappointed it was not "the rat faced" man.

"I can't give you a name, but I've seen him before," Davis told the officer and the attendant standing nearby. He spent the next few minutes trying to tell the stunned state policeman the story of what had happened over the past few weeks including the dead man's part in it. By the time he was finished, the puzzled lawman stood with his mouth open probably wondering about Davis' sanity. Davis assured him he could verify the facts with Chief Hanson in Adairsville.

Finding a coffee machine, Davis returned to the waiting room with cups for both him and Deidre. She was glad for the comfort drink thanking him for his thoughtfulness. "Were you able to identify him?" Her curiosity prompted her to ask before Davis volunteered the information.

"Sort of," Davis replied. "I know who he is, but I don't know his name. It was the 'rat faced" man's partner, one of the men who tried to kill me."

"What? Why would he be in Amy's car?"

"Based on what I know about them, I suspect they were taking her to an isolated spot to murder her. The car the witnesses say passed them just before the accident occurred was, no doubt, the other killer.' That was the method they used with me. She must have known they were intending to kill her, so when she saw people on one side of the road she ran off the road on the other side hoping the 'rat faced" man would not dare return for her with witnesses present."

"You think Amy deliberately ran the car off the road?"

"Of course, I don't know for sure, but that is my guess."

"But why would they want to harm her? Isn't it you they are after?"

Davis pulled the sheet of paper from his shirt pocket that Charley had given him just a few hours earlier handing it to Deidre. "Read this," he suggested.

Deidre unfolded the letter and curiously read:

> *My Dearest Davis,*
>
> *I am writing this letter and placing it where you will find it after I'm gone, assuming I do not get enough courage to give you this information while I am still breathing. I suppose it would not be a disaster if you never knew the news I have to share with you, but I believe it is something you should know. Everyone has a right to know who he is.*

Just a few weeks before she died Mary told me a shocking story.

According to her, she wasn't just my foster mother, she was my birth mother.

The parents I knew in my childhood adopted me out of the Methodist Children's home when I was an infant. They took me to live in Pennsylvania never telling me they were not my real parents. Evidently Mary knew the superintendent of the home. Because of that she had been able to keep tabs on me through the first years of my life, but I am getting ahead of myself.

The fact that hurt me most was that Mary tried to do away with me when I was born. She had somehow been able to keep her pregnancy a secret right up until my birth. She was an unmarried teenager, scared to death. She delivered me leaving me in a cemetery as if nothing had happened.

She told me that what she did almost drove her crazy in the years that followed.

When Mary learned that my adoptive father had taken his own life and eighteen months later my adoptive mother died, she somehow arranged for her and John to become my foster parents.

What she did to me at birth was a terrible thing. When I first found out about it I was furious, but then I remembered that she was a good mother to me for most of my life. I'm glad to say that I was able to forgive her before she went to be with the Lord.

You may have heard the story of Dixie Adair. I guess I am Dixie Adair.

I want you to know that you have been my pride and joy. No mother could love a son more than I love you, and it has brought abundant joy to my heart knowing that love is mutual. I have been truly a blessed woman.

With all my love,
Your Mother

"I still don't understand." Deidre looked at Davis with a puzzled expression. "What does this have to do with those two men trying to kill Amy?"

"This letter is no doubt what Ed Hagan wanted to show me. It, at least, introduces the possibility that Mom was Judson Reed's daughter making me his grandson and Amy his great granddaughter. If that is true, I am heir to the remainder of his fortune. That means the other heir needs to get rid of both me and Amy. With the two of us out of the way, he or she stands to get it all."

"It doesn't seem possible that anyone could do all these horrible things for all the money in the world."

"Oh, there are plenty of people on this planet who would do much more for less," Davis exclaimed.

"Do you have any idea who the other heir is?"

"I don't know yet, not for sure, but I'm going to find out."

Deidre dozed on and off through the remaining hours until dawn. Davis got no sleep. There would be time to sleep when he was sure Amy was out of danger.

At seven o'clock a.m. they went to the hospital cafeteria for coffee. Deidre had some toast. Davis, knowing he needed to get something in his stomach, ate a muffin with his cup of coffee. They would be allowed to see Amy at eight-thirty.

Charley was waiting for them when they got back to the seating area. "I decided to run by to see how things are before I go on duty," he explained.

"We have received no news of any changes", Davis informed his policeman friend. Charley had already gotten the word concerning the identity of the man killed in the crash. Davis shared with him his theory of how Amy had ended up in her present condition. "Do you think you could persuade someone to post an officer to guard her? The 'rat faced' man is still out there somewhere. I have no doubt he will try again."

"I feel sure we can get that done. I will get on it immediately. At least the Rome force is larger than ours. They have more man power available for such duty. Call me if you need me for anything," Charley instructed before leaving to start his shift.

Davis was anxious to see Amy, but at the same time dreaded it. He despised seeing her in her present battered condition. It was almost nine o'clock before they were allowed to visit her. Davis had learned during his years of ministry that visitation in intensive care is often delayed by emergencies or the admission of critical patients. He was beginning to get a little uneasy by the time the announcement was made over the intercom that family members would now be permitted to visit.

Deidre offered to wait until his visit with Amy was over before entering the room, but he took her hand leading her into the room. Davis felt helpless standing beside Amy's bed. He had always taken care of her, from the time she was an infant, he was there to satisfy her needs, and often her whims. There didn't seem to be anything he could do to change this situation. He felt as helpless as he had ever felt in his life. He took her hand in both of his own. "Amy, its Dad. Deidre and I are here to visit with you. Can you hear me, honey?"

Suddenly Davis was sure he could feel Amy trying to squeeze his hand. "Amy, love, can you hear me?" Again he felt a slight squeeze. "Deidre, she is squeezing my hand. I am sure she can hear me." A few moments later Davis excitedly told a nurse what happened. She seemed to feel it was a positive sign. Davis left the room more encouraged than when he entered. "I really feel she is going to be fine." His optimism had a positive affect on Deidre's outlook. Davis saw her smile for the first time since they had entered the hospital. He liked seeing her smile.

Jay arrived mid-morning disappointed that he was not allowed to see Amy immediately. The next opportunity for visitation would be at one-thirty. Davis and Deidre tried to prepare him for what he would find when he did see her. Davis did his best to explain to Jay what he thought had happened. Jay stared at him in disbelief; it was too much like a made for TV movie to believe! "How could anyone intentionally hurt Amy?"

Pastor John arrived not long before eleven o'clock with a big smile on his face. He received an update. The four of them talked for a time mostly about Amy. They laughed together when the preacher shared a humorous story about miscommunication between Amy and the worship leader on a recent Sunday morning when she was at the organ. John's presence along with his positive attitude encouraged the three people who loved Amy most. The four of them joined hands spending some time praying together before John had to leave in order to keep an appointment back in Adairsville. Davis had been touched most by Jay's prayer for his future wife. He realized he had taken the fact that Amy had chosen a Christian to marry for granted. Now his heart was filled with appreciation that they could approach God's throne together to ask for healing mercies.

It was around noon when Tracie appeared. "I came as soon as I heard," she told Davis while giving Deidre a look that said, *I know what you are trying to do.*

"It's good to see you. I didn't know you had returned from your trip to Cincinnati," he said as they embraced.

"I got back yesterday."

"You remember Deidre, and this is Jay, Amy's fiancé."

"Good to meet you, Jay," she said with a smile as she took his hand. "..And it is good to see you again Deidre."

"How is Amy?"

"We don't really know. She is still in a coma, but she did squeeze my hand when we were in to see her this morning. I think she knows what is going on around her."

"When will you see her again?"

"The next scheduled visitation is one-thirty."

"That gives us time to go for a quick lunch. I bet you haven't eaten a thing since you have been here," she said. "Would you two like to join us?" she asked Jay and Deidre in a tone that was less than inviting.

"I think I will get a sandwich here at the hospital," Deidre replied.

"Me too," Jay said. "I want to stay near Amy."

"We will be back soon," Davis told them as he walked away with Tracie at his side not really wanting to go. Tracie drove them to a nearby fast food restaurant where they ate and visited. They were back at the hospital before the announced visitation time.

Tracie let him out of the car at the curb in front of the hospital. "Call me if there is any change."

When Davis hurried back into the hospital he did not find Jay and Deidre where he had left them. He inquired at the desk being told by the lady there that the doctor had appeared a few minutes before to take them back to intensive care. Davis' heart missed a beat or two. Knowing it was not yet time for scheduled visitation, he naturally assumed the worst."

"I'm her father, may I go on back?"

"I'll take you," she offered. She pushed the button to open the double doors. "Come with me."

Every step seemed to be more painful than the one before as the terrified Davis followed the lady in white through the doors and down the hallway.

Chapter 26

When Davis entered the room, Jay was standing on one side of the bed and Deidre the other. Both had wide smiles on their faces. Deidre turned to see who had entered the room; Davis caught a glimpse of Amy, her eyes swollen but open and focused on him. "Hi, Dad," she said in almost a matter of fact tone. Her voice was slower and softer than normal.

"Amy, sweetie! Thank God you are awake?"

"They were trying to kill me, Dad."

"I know, love," he said bending over her to lightly kiss her forehead. "I know, but you are safe now. There is a policeman just outside your door. He will stay there as long as you are here."

"Why, Dad? Why did they want to harm me?"

"We'll talk about that later. The important thing now is that you get well."

They were allowed to stay with Amy for only a couple of minutes longer. The doctor informed them they would need to keep her in intensive care at least until the following morning and then, if all went well, she would be transferred to a private room. Until then they could see her at the scheduled visitation times. Several telephone calls were made giving updates on Amy's condition. Davis learned Tracie had not yet reached home, but he left the message on with her answering service. He caught Charley at the station. "That is great news," Charley said with a sigh of relief. "I don't know if I should be releasing information, so you will want to keep this to yourself. Using the dead man's false IDs we have determined that he was probably Clive Beck from Cincinnati. In the past he has worked with a man named Ramón Garrett also from Cincinnati. Garrett's description sounds like the 'rat faced man'. He has done some prison time, but apparently not nearly as much as he deserves. He obviously is a vicious killer who needs to be put away for life."

"I could have told you that several weeks ago. Do you think Garrett will remain in the area without a partner or will he head for Cincinnati or parts unknown?"

"Who knows, but I would guess he is a vindictive sort of thug. You have gotten away from him twice and Amy once. He may take it person-ally. I wouldn't assume he has gone anywhere even with the heat on."

"I appreciate you arranging the guard for Amy. That is going to be a permanent arrangement isn't it?"

"There will be someone from the Rome police force watching her as long as she is at the hospital. I will personally escort her home when she is dismissed. We will immediately take over guard duty at home. I am hopeful we will wrap this thing up before then. As soon as we have pic-tures of Garrett in hand, we will be hitting the motels, gas station, restau-rants, bars and everywhere else such a person might have gone. If he's around, we'll get him soon."

"I'm counting heavy on that. Thanks for all your help."

Staying at the hospital until he was allowed to again see his daughter, Davis was encouraged by his fifteen minute stay with her. She was more alert than she had been in the last visit, and with a nurse's help was even able to walk a few steps around the room. He and Deidre left for Adairsville shortly after the visit. Jay went to a motel near the hospital. All the way home, Davis regularly glanced into the rear view mirror expecting to dis-cover a car following them. *This is ridiculous, he decided. I can't live the rest of my life looking over my shoulder.* He saw nothing out of the ordinary.

Deidre's support throughout the ordeal left Davis with a strong feeling of gratitude for the mature young woman. Her presence had been a source of encouragement and strength for him. He knew he needed to tell her that, but the words never came. At this particular time, verbalization didn't seem so important to either. Somehow they both understood that the other knew. They were too tired to communicate with words. That would come later. Davis walked Deidre to her door. "Make sure the dead bolt is locked. Call me if there are any problems," he instructed as he waited for her to unlock her door and enter. She flashed a tired smile his way as she closed the door.

Going straight to bed, Davis slept, but restlessly. Sometime during the night or early morning he began to have a series of strange dreams with most of them including Julie. In one of those dreams he was hanging onto a limb on the side of a mountain with his feet dangling. He was about to fall to what would surely be his death. Then he looked up where Julie stood on the ledge above him. All was not lost Julie was there. She would somehow save him. She was always there when he needed her. He looked down and then upward. Julie was gone. He was losing his grip and Julie was no longer there. *Julie, Where are you? I need you! Help me!* In his dream Davis could hold on no longer and then he was falling rapidly crying out to Julie.

Davis awoke in a cold sweat, so much so that he had to flip his pillow over because the side on which his head had been laying was wringing wet. He thought about his dream wishing that Julie had not left him. He needed her now more than ever. As he lay there he remembered a conversation he had with her not long before her death. Perhaps he had not remembered it before because he had shut it out of his mind.

They were alone, she lying on her back on her hospital bed, him in a chair at her side. She reached for his hand trying her best to smile through the pain. "Thank you", she said looking into her husband's eyes.

"For what?" Davis asked.

"For the life we have had together. It has been a good life, everything I ever wanted; you are the one who made it possible. You are a strong person Davis Morgan, much stronger than you think you are. That strength will serve you and Amy well when I am gone. You are going to need a partner in the years ahead. I have been praying that the Lord will give you someone you can love like you have loved me, someone who will love you as I love you."

Davis remembered his response. "You are my one and only love," he told her. Remembering, he wiped away the tears running down his cheeks.

After lying awake for some time Davis finally dosed again. The alarm awakened him at six-thirty. Resting there for a few minutes, he realized he seemed more tired than he had been when he had finally gotten to bed. No amount of manual labor could come close to producing the kind of exhaustion that results from emotional stress.

Spending a little time straightening up his neglected apartment, Davis took time out later in the morning to make a call to a preacher friend who now lived in Cincinnati. They had become acquainted when they both lived in Indianapolis. He asked his friend Walter to go to the library to look for some five year old information. Walter assured him he would get back to him as soon as possible.

Charley went with Davis to visit Amy in the early afternoon. She had been transferred to a private room which was a blessing since it would enable them to be with her more constantly. It was also a positive sign of her progress. They found Deidre already there along with Jay. For the first time, Davis talked with Amy about specifics concerning the attempt on her life. Amy confirmed part of Davis' theory.

"I didn't know what else to do," she told them. "I knew they were going to kill me. They made that clear from the time I was abducted. The shorter of the two, the one you call the 'rat faced' man, said something about making the motive look like rape. I didn't know what they would do to me before they shot me." Amy's voice broke. "When I saw several people in that yard, I decided my only chance was to get their attention. I reached up to honk the horn. The man beside me must have realized what I was going to try to do and grabbed my arm. I guess the car went out of control. I don't remember anything after that. I can't believe he is dead."

Not wanting Amy to feel guilt about her captor's death Davis explained, "People who choose to live a life of vicious crime rarely die well. Remember he is the same person who killed or aided in murdering Ed Hagan and Mr. Brown. He almost succeeded in helping to kill both you and me. There is no telling how many people he has hurt or how many lives he has taken. You are not responsible for his death. You have no reason to feel guilty."

"But I do not understand why they thought they had to kill me. What possible threat could I be to them?"

"They think you and I are heirs to the fortune I told you about. With us out of the way, the person for whom they are obviously working stands to inherit a lot of money."

"Why would they think we are the heirs?"

"I might as well show you this now." Davis pulled the letter from his mother out of his shirt pocket. "Charley brought it to me the day you were abducted. I was trying to reach you to let you see it".

He held it out to give it to her. Amy shook her head. "Maybe you ought to read it to me. My vision is still blurred."

Before reading the letter, he explained that it had come out of Ed Hagan's safety deposit box and that the handy man had probably found it when he was working at their place. "My guess is he found it in the attic when he was cleaning there. I probably innocently put it up there back when I put the contents of the dresser drawers in boxes after your grandmother's death."

After listening to her Father read the letter, Amy remained silent for a few moments before commenting. "The letter says nothing about who grandmother's father was. This doesn't prove anything."

"You are right, it doesn't. Probably Ed and whoever is behind all this reasoned it was too much to be a coincidence. The time of Mom's birth and the time that any child Judson Reed would have fathered while in Adairsville would be very close. Mr. Brown may have had more information, but I guess we will never know. You don't worry about that killer coming back after you. There is a policeman outside your door at all times."

"Do you have any idea who is behind all this?" Amy asked.

"No, not for sure," he answered. "But we are going to find out."

"What do you mean 'we,'" Charley who had been silently listening closely inquired. "You got something in mind? I strongly suggest you leave the detective work to the police. You do recall what happened on Cape Cod?"

"Yeah, I remember. You got shot in the leg," Davis replied. Immediately realizing his words and tone were inappropriate, Davis apologized to his young friend, "I'm sorry, Charley. You got shot saving my life, and no one could appreciate your police skills more than I do. It's just that everything that has happened over the past weeks is making me crazy. I've never had to deal with such violence. I've never come so close to being killed, and now I have come within an inch of losing my little girl." For a few moments Davis had forgotten the other people in the room and the need for optimism for their sakes.

"You are right, Charley. You guys do your job well, and you are going to get these people. I know it!"

"You can count on it!" Charley told him.

Later in the day, after returning home, Davis received the call from Cincinnati for which he had been waiting. The information his friend gave him was not news he was happy about receiving. After hanging up, he sat silently for a few minutes staring straight ahead. He finally rose driving to his shop. There was work to be done there, but keeping his mind on his chores was impossible. He eventually gave up and drove to the cemetery where he visited Julie's grave. After a few minutes he got back into his car starting home. After going inside he pulled out his cell phone punching Tracie's number.

"Tracie, this is Davis. I would very much like to see you this evening. Could we meet at the Inn for dinner?"

"I have another engagement, but I think I can get out of it. If you will give me a few minutes to make a call, I'll get back to you as soon as possible."

"I would appreciate it. There is nothing in particular. I just need to see you."

Tracie called ten minutes later with news she had been able to make arrangements to free herself to be with him for the evening. "I'll meet you at the restaurant at seven o'clock," she told him.

Concentration was a problem when Davis tried to read. He found himself having to reread almost every paragraph he read. He finally gave up closing his book and laying his head on the back of the chair he closed his eyes for a few minutes. Shortly thereafter he heard Deidre enter her apartment. He walked around to her front door where she let him in after hearing him knock. "I thought I would let you know I will be out for awhile tonight. I know it must be scary for you staying in the house alone in light of everything that has happened, but I do need to be out for a while. It is sort of important. You may want to get someone to stay with you while I am away."

"I'll be all right," she assured him. "I'll probably be the safest person in town with the police keeping such a close watch on this place."

"Please take all the precautions," he told her. "I'll be just across the railroad tracks at the Inn if you need me. You have my cell number. Don't hesitate to call 911 if you feel anything is wrong."

"I'll do that. You go and try to relax. Don't worry about me. Are you having dinner with Tracie?" She asked trying not to sound disappointed, but failing in that effort.

"Yes, she is going to meet me there at seven o'clock, but I'll be home early. I think Amy is looking great, don't you?" He was sincere, but the comment was made to change the subject.

"She is going to be fine. Jay is with her constantly. I think that is helping to speed up her recovery. In a few days she will be on her feet going full steam ahead as she gets ready for the wedding. You don't keep a bundle of energy like Amy down for very long."

"I'm sure you are right. He is good for her isn't he? It has taken me a while to realize that, but I am thrilled that she has found someone who makes her happy, someone who shares her faith. I'm glad he can be with her through these early stages of recovery. Love has a way of quickly healing the hurt that comes into our lives."

Deidre smiled at that statement responding, "Amen, brother."

Returning to his living quarters, Davis changed from jeans into blue blazer, gray slacks, white shirt and considered a gray and red striped tie before deciding on the open collar look. He arrived at the restaurant early, taking the opportunity to briefly visit with several people he knew during the almost half hour he waited for Tracie. Davis enjoyed a visit with Ralph Hayes and his wife along with two other couples from the Crown Creek Church. They informed him that they had a good pastor prospect for their church, one of the young men he had recommended. Davis hoped it worked out. He would be happy to have the young man who happened to be a "Timothy" of his in the community. Most of the people to whom he spoke while waiting inquired about Amy's recovery. He was glad to give them the good report.

Tracie was as beautiful as usual, dressed to the hilt. Her personality was such that she caused a room to come alive simply by walking into it. Davis decided that it was her energy and obvious zest for living that made her so appealing. Of course, her beauty, highlighted by those little girl dimples, didn't hurt either.

"Hi, honey," she said moving quickly toward him. She took both of his hands standing on her tip toes to kiss him on the cheek. They were shown to their table by the hostess. They did not have to wait very long for the waitress to take their order.

"I was feeling a little out of it," he told her. "I just knew seeing you would help get me out of the doldrums."

"Well, you came to the right place. I'll do everything I can to cheer you up."

"You already have. My mood took a turn for the better when you walked into the room."

"That's the sort of thing a girl likes to hear, but then you are always saying things that are nice to the ears."

"I'm afraid I haven't been myself recently. Guns, bombs, and violence are new to me, and I'm afraid it doesn't bring out my best. I'm accustomed to going and coming as I please. Having a policeman looking over my shoulder telling me what I can and cannot do hasn't been good for my disposition. It causes me to feel confined."

"Maybe just the two of us could get away somewhere. No policemen, no bad guys, no hospitals, just the two of us together. I am sure I can make you forget it all."

"It's a tempting offer, and I am sure you could, but I don't want to risk your life. I think I'm going to sneak off in the morning by myself to spend a few hours on Fort Mountain. It has always been one of my favorite spots, and I can get there in little over an hour. Not a lot of travel time to get there. If I'm careful, making sure no one follows me, I'll be safe. I've always enjoyed the mountain. I can spend long periods of time atop the tower just enjoying the beauty of nature around me. There is hardly anybody who goes up there this time of the year. I can get there around ten thirty or eleven, spend two or three hours and still get back here by mid-afternoon."

"Sounds like a good plan. I think it would be good for you. I wish I could go with you, but I understand and appreciate your caution."

"I wish it were possible for you to make the trip. That would make it a perfect day. We'll take a picnic lunch as soon as all of this is settled."

"That would be a lot of fun. I'll be looking forward to it."

Their dinners came quickly. They ate, talked, and Davis, remembering his promise to Deidre, arrived back at his apartment between eight thirty and nine. The night was long. Davis had been lonely for a while, but he didn't remember being more lonely than he was now. He thought about picking up his cell to call Deidre, but decided he did not want to disturb her in the middle of the night. He slept very little. Psalm 30:10 repeated in his mind through the night. "*Hear, O Lord, and be merciful to me; O Lord, be my help.*" Some time early morning before dawn he remarked to himself. *Maybe all this will come to an end, one way or another today.* The thought greatly encouraged him; however, he knew there was always the possibility it would not end well.

Chapter 27

———◆✕◆———

Getting up well before dawn Davis dressed in jeans, golf-shirt, sneakers, and baseball cap; he telephoned Deidre. "Deidre, I'm sorry to wake you so early. I'll explain all of this later. May I borrow your car for the day? I promise I will take good care of it."

"Sure," she said in a voice as clear as if it were the middle of the day. That reminded Davis of Julie. He needed to be up for a couple of hours before he sounded normal. Julie could get up in the middle of the night and sound perfectly awake.

"Also, would you move my car behind the house about nine-thirty. Put it in the back where it cannot be seen, but be sure to wait until about nine-thirty."

"I'll do it, but I would like to know what you are up to."

"There is nothing to worry about," he said. "I think its best you don't know. I'll be around in a moment to get your keys. Don't turn on the porch light."

Davis didn't own a gun. Julie had always been afraid to have one in the house, and he had no particular interest in them himself. He did have a baseball bat, a thirty-three inch Louisville Slugger that went back to his middle teen years when he played summer American legion ball in Calhoun. It had a small handle and a big barrel, an official Hank Aaron model with which he had hit a few home runs as a youngster. He took it out of the closet before leaving the house with it in his hand. He tried to hide the bat when Deidre in a bulky white robe opened the door to exchange keys. His attempt was unsuccessful.

Looking at the bat and then at him with a puzzled look on her face Deidre spoke in a tone that gave away some of her concern. "I'm not even going to ask," she said. "I guess I will just have to have faith that you know what you are doing and that the Lord will watch over you. Be careful," she exhorted. Kissing him on the cheek she quickly turned to go back inside.

A young policeman who Davis did not know well was in front of the house in the patrol car. Davis was more convinced than ever that he was doing the right thing when he had to knock on the window of the passenger side to wake the officer. "I'm going to be gone for a while, but I want you to keep an eye on the young lady in the house."

The officer, still half asleep, nodded offering no resistance to the plan. Davis remembering something he had forgotten made a quick trip back into the house. He returned with a roll of duct tape. He got behind the wheel of Deidre's small Chevy, throwing the duct tape onto the seat next to him. He propped the bat handle up, between the passenger seat and the door. He didn't want it rolling around in the car. It took Davis only a couple of minutes to drive from his house to I-75. He went north, taking the exit that was marked "Chatsworth".

Deidre started praying when Davis drove her car from their driveway onto Railroad Street. *Lord I don't know what he has in mind, but I know whatever it is likely will be dangerous. Protect him and keep him from harm. May he sense your presence throughout the day….*

Mentally kicking herself Deidre questioned, *should I have tried to stop him? He probably would not have listened to anything I had to say, but I didn't even try. What if something happens to him? He would never know how I feel, how important he is to me.* She got up from the chair where she had flopped when Davis left her. Breakfast was not appealing, but she made coffee and toast anyway. She sat down at the table occasionally sipping from the cup and nibbling on the toast.

Deidre made her bed neat enough to pass inspection in a military barracks. Her heart was not in the vacuuming, dusting, and the kitchen cleanup which she initiated next, but she knew that for her own well being she needed to keep busy. At nine-thirty she went outside, moving Davis' car behind the house making sure it was where it could not be seen by anyone passing by. She wondered why that was necessary, but she did as she had been instructed.

The telephone was ringing when Deidre returned to the living room. She heard a familiar voice when she picked up the handset. "Deidre, this is Amy. Lying here in bed hour after hour gets old. I need to talk with someone to maintain my sanity. Do you have some time?"

"Sure, I have all the time you need. I was getting a little lonesome myself," she told her roommate.

"Do you know where Dad has gone? I couldn't get him at home or at the shop, and he doesn't answer his cell phone."

Deidre knew she dared not tell Amy that her father had left early in a very serious frame of mind with a baseball bat in his hand. "No, I don't know where he is," she honestly stated.

"I worry he will do something that will get him hurt or worst. I didn't like the mood he was in when he was here yesterday. He tried to hide it, but there is not much he can keep from me. He seemed a little down."

"You don't need to worry about your dad," Deidre said trying as much to convince herself as Amy. "There is no one more level headed than Davis Morgan. You can count on him to stay out of trouble. He'll be okay. Where is Jay?" She asked in a desperate attempt to change the subject.

"He had to make some business calls this morning before leaving the motel. He should be here soon."

"Did you two make any wedding decisions last night?" There was a design behind Deidre's question. She did not want to answer any more inquiries Amy might make as to Davis' activity. She did not like misleading her friend even for her own good. Introducing the wedding subject into the conversation would be a sure way to keep Amy's mind off anything else. The plan worked perfectly as Amy talked a mile a minute about the special day coming up the last part of August. When the young woman on the other end of the line paused Deidre simply asked another question about the wedding.

They talked for almost an hour at which time their conversation ended when Amy announced, "Deidre I'm going to have to go. Jay is here."

Davis drove past New Echota, the restored Cherokee Capitol where the Cherokees had published their own newspaper before their removal to the Oklahoma territory. Passing those buildings reminded Davis of one of the most glaring injustices in American history. Twenty minutes later, he passed the Chief Van house. A large brick house built by a half-blood Cherokee just after 1800 providing further proof that the Cherokee were not a tribe of ignorant savages. Pre-removal Cherokee history fascinated

Davis. It was an interest he hoped to pursue with some serious research when the current difficulties were cleared up. *Maybe that will be today.* The thought added to the sense of urgency he felt about the day's mission causing him to speed up a bit.

Chatsworth was still asleep when Davis passed through the charming county seat of Murray County. The earliest stage of sunrise in the east was visible through his windshield. He checked his fuel gage before starting the climb up the mountain. *No place to buy gas up there,* he decided looking at the imposing sight in front of him. Gas was not a problem. The tank was well over half full. Only minutes later he was pulling through the gate of the state park.

Fort Mountain or Chatsworth Mountain, it is known by both names, was given to the state by a prominent Georgia citizen in the early nineteen thirties. The fact that it is one of the highest points in the state isn't its only appeal. There is a mysterious stone wall that runs for some distance near the top of the mountain. No one has ever been able to solve the mystery behind its origin. The popular theory when Davis was a boy was that Desoto and his men had built it when they passed through, but since it is now known that Desoto was in the area for a very short period of time, that theory was ruled out. Other theories range from a Welch explorer in the fifteen hundreds to the possibility that it was some kind of honeymoon haven for newly wed Native Americans. More likely than not, it had been built by one tribe as protection against another.

The stone tower is just beyond the mysterious wall at the very top of the mountain. It was built by Roosevelt's C.C.C boys back in the late nineteen thirties or very early forties. In order to get to the tower, it would be necessary to park the car and walk along a steep trail for approximately a mile. Davis chose a parking place well beyond where the trail started. As he had anticipated, there were no other cars in the lot. Fort Mountain still had not been discovered by most people in Georgia, and, in the late spring, early summer few people came. This early in the day, the chance of anyone else being there would be extremely slim.

Taking his baseball bat and duct tape, Davis locked the car door walking back to where the trail to the wall and tower started. The climb up the steep mountain had Davis huffing and puffing. He decided he must start running again when all of this is resolved. He came to the wall where he stopped to read the historical marker, but had to admit to himself that it was actually to catch his breath. He had read the marker several times previously. A short distance farther up the trail, he saw the stone tower rising more than sixty feet high. He climbed the winding wooden stairs to the top. From his perch on the platform, it would be possible to have a clear view of anyone coming up the trail long before they reached the top.

The stone wall of the tower rose approximately four feet above the platform on top, which meant the safety wall rose to just about Davis' waist. He sat on the wall where he could keep a close watch on the trail patiently waiting. During this time of inactivity his mind began to question his course of action. *Do I have the right to engage in violence against another human being? I dare not forget that this man is God's child, God's creation, but he is also a murderer. He must be stopped before he takes the life of others including my own daughter's,* he reasoned. *Is that sound Biblical logic or is it shallow rationalization? I don't intend to do him any serious harm.* Deep down Davis knew he was being naive. If the encounter did indeed take place, he didn't know what course of action would be required. *This was the worst sort of villain. He certainly will not lay down his gun and raise his hands when he spots me here on the platform with my baseball bat.* Davis was now having trouble justifying the course of action he had chosen.

Then there is the question of how this will turn out. Davis asked himself, *am I ready to die if this doesn't go the way I planned? I know I would go to be with the Lord and that is a good thing, but there is Amy to consider. It has been just a year since she lost her mother. How could she cope with losing still another parent so soon?* Davis' hands were damp as he took his handkerchief from his back pocket mopping the perspiration from his forehead. He didn't have Julie to help him find answers to all those questions, but he knew there was One with him at that moment who had the answers, One that he had somewhat neglected recently.

He quietly prayed: "Lord, you know my dilemma. Am I out of bounds on this one? Have I gotten ahead of You by taken matters into my own hands? I know I am prone to do that. On the other hand, I know You use people to do Your work. I need to know what You want me to do. If I am going to face this man head on I need to be sure it is Your will. I need Your strength. I can't do it on my own..."

After a time Davis' mind went to one of the earliest Bible stories he learned as a child, the account of David and Goliath. The shepherd boy, David, was clearly doing the work of God when he, with his sling and three smooth stones, went down into the valley to do battle with the giant. Davis knew he was no David and the "rat faced" man was no Goliath, but the principle seemed to him to be the same. In his mind Davis quoted the first verse from Psalm 30, a reference he did not even know he had committed to memory. "*I will exalt you, O Lord, for you lifted me out of the depths and did not let my enemies gloat over me.*" *I am ready to be lifted out of the depths,* Davis decided.

Garrett, unfamiliar with the Georgia state park called Fort Mountain, made a couple of wrong turns before finally finding his way up the mountain through the park gate. He saw only two parked cars as he pulled into the parking lot and neither was Morgan's. He had been afraid his mark had gotten ahead of him while he was trying to find his way, but evidently he was still on target. He took the hand gun lying on the seat beside him sticking it in the waist band of his pants. Even though it was a warm day, he put on the sports jacket he had brought in order to conceal the gun. It took him only a few moments to find the trail marked "Tower". He walked in that direction having been told that would be Morgan's destination.

This time I've got him for sure! It's the perfect plan. I'll hide on the tower until he arrives, plug him and leave him where he falls. I will decide how to handle anyone else who might be around if that becomes a problem, he decided.

After walking for a while Garrett was finding it hard to climb the steep trail. The loose rocks caused him to slip and slide. He wished he had worn shoes that were more conducive to this kind of activity. *I didn't know I was going to have to climb a mountain to get this job done and I will get it done this time.* The hardened killer lamented the fact that he was having such a difficult time completing this contract. *The boss hasn't been happy with me. It is like those people have some kind of supernatural bubble protecting them. They have been lucky so far, but I'll take care of Morgan today. It won't be hard to get the girl as soon as she is dismissed from the hospital. I'll be glad when it is over and I can get out of this uncivilized, back woods corner of the world. It will be good to get back to the city. The south is definitely not my cup of tea.*

Two people, a middle aged man and a woman, were coming toward him. He knew if they saw his face clearly they might be able to identify him later so he turned to his left to walk off the trail until they passed.

He walked approximately a hundred and fifty feet making sure he kept his back to them until they disappeared. On his way back to the trail he stepped over a fallen log being startled by a three foot long black snake that slithered past his feet. It took all the will power he had to keep him from pulling his gun from his waist band to blow the snake to kingdom come. *I've got to get this job done and get out of here;* he decided pulling his handkerchief out of his back pocket to wipe the sweat off his forehead as he watched the snake disappear into a thick growth of bushes. He wondered how many more snakes were between him and the tower,

Up ahead Garrett could see the tower. *Almost there. Another hundred yards and I'll be in place for the kill. Maybe I've got enough left to make it up the stairs to the top. I'm sure I'll have some time to rest before Morgan gets here,* he reasoned while breathing hard. *He is not due for a while yet.*

After a long wait Davis was starting to think his scheme was going to produce no results. He almost hoped it didn't. One middle aged couple came up the trail, climbed the stairs, and remained on the top platform with him for less than five minutes obviously enjoying the view before making their way back toward the parking lot. After they had been gone for about ten minutes Davis caught a glimpse of someone in the distance, a man alone coming toward him. He ducked to lower himself below the wall. He kept his head just high enough to watch the stumbling hiker. The approaching figure was often obscured by the leaves but occasional flashes indicated his steady progress. As he got closer, Davis felt his pulse speed up. It was him! The "rat faced" man would soon be on the tower.

After a few moments had passed, Davis could hear his adversary's foot steps as he climbed the stairs. He was counting on the killer being out of shape. He hoped his long rest would give him an edge over the man who had just hiked a mile up a steep trail and climbed a lot of steps to get to the top platform. He also knew he had the element of surprise on his side. The "rat faced" man was not expecting him to arrive for a while yet. No doubt, it was his plan to wait at the top of the tower for Davis to come to him.

Holding the baseball bat as a left handed hitter would hold it with his feet about a yard apart, Davis got into position to the left of the entrance. He would be only a couple of feet from the killer as he stepped onto the upper level. He was tense, for a moment doubting he could pull this thing off, but knowing at this point there was no turning back. He would carry out his plan or die. Those were the only two choices he had. Davis could hear the man's steps getting closer, and then he appeared.

"Are you looking for me?" Davis cried out.

The "rat faced man" was taken by total surprise. For a moment he stood frozen. Then he reached across his body with his right hand. Davis, guessing he was reaching for a gun tucked in the waste band of his pants, swung the bat as hard as he was capable, aiming for the man's right shoulder. He connected at precisely the moment the gun was pulled. There was a "thud" and the "rat faced" man cried out in pain. The gun fell to the deck about three feet in front of the grimacing figure who grabbed his shoulder falling to his knees. His eyes focused on the gun. He dove, trying to scoop up the weapon with his left hand. Davis, still holding the bat, jumped with both feet on the man's hand and wrist. "You touch that gun and the next time I will swing for your head," Davis yelled, not sure he could actually intentionally do anything to critically injure another human being, even the "rat faced" man.

The fight seemed to be gone from the murderer who now was lying face down on the deck. Davis cautiously holding the bat over his adversary's head with his right hand reached down picking up the gun with his left. "Stay where you are," he commanded. Davis pointed the pistol toward his defeated victim. "Stand up and put your hands behind you."

Getting to his feet, the "rat faced" man whined as he attempted to follow Davis' orders to put his hands behind him. "That hurts. I think you broke my shoulder."

"I am truly sorry for your pain, but I want you to put your hands behind you." When Davis saw how difficult it was for the man to get his right hand behind him, there was a moment of sympathy that almost caused him to relinquish the order. Then he remembered who he was dealing with. He knew he could take no chances. Davis held the gun in his left hand while he struggled to tape the man's hands behind him with his one free hand. He made a conscientious effort not to hurt the animal who had tried to kill him and his daughter. Having finished that task to his satisfaction, he instructed the "rat faced" man to get up and start down the stairs of the tower and then toward the trail. He walked three or four feet behind him, pointing the gun toward his prisoner while holding his baseball bat in his left hand. About half way to the parking lot they met four people, two couples, headed up the trail. The look on their faces ran from fear to puzzlement. It occurred to Davis that what they were seeing looked like something out of an old John Wayne movie. As he passed the people, who for a moment had completely stopped walking, he smiled. "Don't worry, folks. I'm the good guy. Enjoy your day." As Davis glanced back he saw that one of the ladies had taken out a cell phone and was rapidly talking into it. All four members of the group were focused on him and his prisoner.

When they got to the car, Davis opened the trunk lid. "Get in," he commanded!

Garrett objected. "You aren't going to make me ride in there?"

"Oh yes, I am. It's the only safe way to go. I said get in!"

With his hands behind him, the "rat faced" man struggled to get in the trunk. It was accomplished only with the captor's help. Davis taped his prisoner's ankles together before he closed the lid. Starting the drive back to Adairsville Davis knew the killer would be in no real danger as the result of his short ride in the trunk.

Charley spent most of the morning covering the town of Adairsville looking for his friend, Davis. He had gone to all the bookseller's regular hangouts questioning his known associates and acquaintances without success. He approached Deidre who told him that her land lord had left early this morning in her car carrying a baseball bat. He knew Davis was up to something. He hoped whatever it was would not cost him his life. Tom, the newest officer on the force, could lose his badge for letting Davis leave without an escort. He hoped for Tom's sake as well as Davis' that his elusive friend was found unharmed soon. *He is a survivor.* Charley's observation about Davis didn't make him feel any better.

I hope nothing has happened to that crazy preacher. He pondered his unlikely friendship with the former pastor turned bookseller. *Actually he is Dean's friend,* he told himself. *He is probably twenty years older than me. We have absolutely nothing in common.* Despite what he was telling himself, the worried policeman knew he had grown extremely fond of this man who had become his constant companion over the past few weeks. Charley could count the number of people he considered true friends on his fingers. Davis was certainly one of them.

When Chief Hanson walked into the station with another officer Charley eagerly questioned him. "Did you find anything?"

"No, not really, Old Jud Smith said he thought he saw Davis in a car that wasn't his entering the interstate going north early this morning, but he wasn't sure. I would not be surprised if we have not seen the last of Davis Morgan. If that killer was able to get his hands on him he is a dead man by now."

Charley wasn't ready to admit that the chief's statement was true, but he did not know what else to do. No stone had been left unturned and still no leads had been found. He felt totally helpless. There was no where else to go. Sitting down at his desk Charley dropped his head as his mind went in an unfamiliar direction. *If I knew anything about prayer now would certainly be the time.* Seldom in his life had Charley felt completely lost for an answer, but this was one of those times. He could think of nothing to do in order to help his friend.

Driving straight to the police station, Davis went inside where he found Chief Hanson and Charley. "Where have you been?" Charley yelled at him.

"We have been looking for you all morning," the chief scolded.

"Oh, I took a trip to Fort Mountain, and guess what I've got? Walk out to the car with me." Davis raised the trunk lid. "Gentlemen, I give you the 'rat faced' man. He is in some pain. You may want to get a doctor to look at his shoulder; otherwise, he is in pretty good shape." As his prisoner was being booked into the jail Davis spent the next half-hour explaining to the two policemen the details of the capture.

"How did you set the trap? I don't understand how he knew you were there if he didn't follow you." Charley looked puzzled.

"All I had to do was let the word get out to the right person. Do you mind if I make a call?" Davis pulled his cell from his pocket.

He punched Deidre's number. "Hello, Deidre, this is Davis. I wanted you to know I'm back in town. The 'rat faced' man is in jail, and I couldn't be better. I'll return your car in a few minutes."

"No hurry," Deidre answered. "I've got just one question I need to ask you." There was an upbeat tone in her voice obviously in an effort to disguise the relief she felt. "Did you have to use the baseball bat?"

"It did come in rather handy. The 'rat faced' man may be a little sore for a few days, but nobody was seriously injured. Would you call Amy and tell her she doesn't have to worry about the killer anymore? He is in the custody of the Adairsville Police Department."

"I'll do it right away. I know that is going to be a load off her mind."

"Thanks, Deidre. I'll see you in a few minutes."

"Hello Tracie, Davis said after punching another number. This is Davis. How has your day been?"

"It has been fine," she responded after a moment of silence. "You are back from the mountain rather soon. Is everything all right?" Tracie spoke as if she were puzzled.

"It couldn't be better. It was a great morning on Fort Mountain. I have a much better outlook on life today than I had this time yesterday. "

"I'm glad. I was worried about you."

"I need just one more thing to make my day perfect. I close the shop at five o'clock. Could you stop in around closing time?"

"Around closing time huh? What do you have in mind?" She laughed.

"I'll tell you when you get there."

"I'll be there with bells on. See you then."

Chapter 28

When Davis returned Deidre's car he took a few minutes to explain to her step by step how he had managed to capture the "rat faced" man. He felt a little like the conquering hero telling the beautiful princess about his heroics. After a while he decided he was coming across a little more macho than he wanted to appear to this young woman whose favor he wanted so very much to maintain. "The truth is I was scared to death the whole time," he finally admitted. "Even when I had him taped up like a mummy and locked in the trunk with his gun beside me, I didn't feel safe until he was in police custody. There is just one more loose end to tie up. Hopefully this time tomorrow we will be able to breathe a little easier."

"I hope so," she said. "There has been a little too much excitement for this small town school teacher. I just want things to get back to a reasonable degree of normality."

"I couldn't agree more. I'm looking forward to spending my days selling books. Perhaps you and Amy will have some time to help me search for books now that you are out of school for the summer with more time on your hands. I suspect Amy will be dismissed from the hospital in a couple of days."

"Amy is probably going to be pretty busy with details for her wedding since it is less than two months away with a lot still to do in order to be ready, but I would love to help you. I really do want to learn more about collecting. I think I could get hooked."

From Deidre's apartment, Davis took his own car to his shop. There was not much going on. Until the final detail was taken care of, he would have difficulty concentrating on his work. He sat down to have a cup of coffee with Janie never mentioning his ordeal earlier in the day. They talked about business passing the time with chit chat. Janie got up to check out a customer. Davis was disappointed to see the customer approach the counter with a handful of linen and a couple of gift items. One of the other tenants would profit from this sale.

When Janie returned to the table Davis tried to casually give her some instructions. "I have someone coming in at closing time. You go on home at five. I will lock up. Be sure to leave the back door, the one over by my shop, unlocked when you leave."

"I'll do whatever you say, kind sir. I am ready to go home. It has been a long day and my feet are killing me. Make sure you check all the lights before you leave, including the bathrooms, and don't forget to adjust the thermostat. It needs to be left on seventy-two."

"Don't worry. I'll take care of everything. Don't want you to get fired. The Corra Harris Bookshop would go under without your energy and expert help."

"You know that's right." She laughed understanding she actually knew about as little as a person could know about books. When time came for Janie to leave, Tracie had not yet arrived. "See you tomorrow, Davis. Have a nice evening." Janie spoke loudly as she walked through the front door to her car. As Davis watched her drive away, Tracie in her shiny red sports car drove into the parking space Janie had vacated directly in front of the Stock Exchange. She got out of her car walking through the front door.

"Come on in, lovely lady," he smiled as she came into the building. "I think you get more beautiful every time I see you."

"Well, thank you. I work hard to make myself beautiful for you, but one does have to have something to start with," she laughed.

"You certainly have that." He assured her continuing the light turn the conversation had taken. "Come into my shop," he suggested. There are a couple of chairs there where we can be comfortable."

She followed him to the two chairs that were placed near the back door. He motioned for her to sit in the larger, more comfortable of the two while he seated himself in the other. "Tell me about your trip this morning," she suggested. "Did anything unusual happen?"

"Oh, you might say that. I hit a man with a ball bat, taped his hands behind him, put him in the trunk of the car and brought him back to the Adairsville police where they locked him away behind bars."

"What?" She suddenly turned pale.

"That is exactly what happened," he went on. "Don't you want to know who it was? But I suppose you have a pretty good idea since I am sure you sent him."

"What are you talking about?" She raised her voice that was already filled with stress.

"You know exactly what I am talking about Tracie, or should I say Cousin Tracie. Isn't that right? It's very possible that we are cousins. I guess that would make us kissing cousins."

"Are you out of your mind? You must have been in the sun too long this morning."

"No, just long enough. I was on the top of that mountain just long enough to put an end to this nightmare. Tell me if I've got it right beautiful lady. You had your husband killed five years ago when you learned you were the only known heir to the Reed fortune. A friend of mine dug around in some old Cincinnati newspapers recently. Guess what he found? Your husband did not die accidentally. He was killed when someone taped his hands behind him and put a gun to his head. Sounds rather familiar doesn't it? Ed Hagan came to you with a letter that might deny you access to the remainder of the fortune. I don't know how he knew about your inheritance or the conditions connected to the remainder of the money, but I suspect it had something to do with Mr. Brown being sent to town to uncover the second heir. While Ed was working for you, he probably listened to your calls or read your mail somehow piecing it all together. Am I right?" Tracie did not answer. She just sat looking at Davis with a stunned look on her face.

"When you refused to give him the money he asked for, he threatened to show my mother's letter to me. You certainly couldn't let that happen, so you had him killed. Naturally you sent for the same men who had killed your husband five years ago in Cincinnati. They had proven they could do the job. They did kill Ed, but they never found the letter, so you, thinking it was in the house, had your thugs blow up Ed's house almost killing Charley and me in the process. Do I have it right so far?"

"You are coming pretty close," Tracie finally broke her silence.

"You knew you had to get me out of the picture. Someone would surely discover that Reed had fathered a second child, my mother, and you would be out a quarter of a billion dollars. So you sent your paid killers after me. Getting reacquainted with me, of course, would put you in a position to know all my movements, making it easier to get the job done. When Mr. Brown was ready to come to me with whatever he had found, you knew you had to have him stopped. Your killers got to him shortly before he got to me, and I was the fool who told you he was coming. Somewhere along the line it occurred to you that even when I was dead there would still be an heir who would keep you from your millions. My daughter would be in line for the inheritance if I were gone. With both of us out of the way, there would be no one to stand in your way. It would be all yours."

"When did you figure it out?" Tracie asked.

"Not until recently. Even though there were clues I should have noticed way back in the beginning. Why did Mr. Brown suggest that he needed to talk with you when we saw him at Barnsley Gardens? That sounded an alarm, but probably because I was so blinded by the attention I was receiving from such a beautiful and desirable woman, I just pushed it aside. He knew you were the first heir. He just wanted your cooperation but you weren't willing to give it to him. When the police finally identified the killers telling me they were from Cincinnati, it started coming together. That is when I contacted my friend there for information about your husband's death. Then it came back to me that I was on my way to pick you up when I was abducted. I told you about Mr. Brown coming to see me, and he was killed before he reached me. You were one of only a handful of people who knew Charley and I were going to Boston where your hired killer almost got the job done. It was just too much to be coincidence."

"And you set me up last night. You told me you were going to Fort Mountain knowing I would send Garrett."

"That's right. I was waiting for him with a baseball bat when he got there."

"You aren't an easy man to kill Davis Morgan. I want you to know it was nothing personal. It may sound strange, but I really do like you a lot. I guess I'm more in love with money and the life style it provides than I could ever be with any man."

"Why couldn't you be satisfied with your half of the inheritance? I don't even know for sure that I am Judson Reed's grandson. My mother's letter doesn't mention who her father was. All we know is she was born to an unmarried girl during the time period that would make it possible for her to be Reed's child."

"Oh, she was his daughter all right. I guess I could never be satisfied with any amount of money as long as there is a possibility of more. I am sure you cannot understand that, but it's just the way I am."

"Yes, and being that way is going to get you the rest of your life in prison or worse."

"Not likely," she replied pulling a small hand gun from the handbag that she undoubtedly opened while Davis was caught up in the conversation. She pointed the gun toward him remarking, "I guess I'm going to have to do Garrett's job myself."

"You would have thought I had learned my lesson by now. I guess I can't help being blinded by that beautiful smile."

At that moment the back door behind Tracie's chair silently opened. "You'd best give the gun to us," the chief suggested with his own pointed at her back. Charlie took the revolver from her hand instantly cuffing her wrists.

"I should have known," she sounded disappointed in herself. "You couldn't prove any of it could you?"

"No, not really, that is until these gentlemen heard your confession a few moments ago."

"I'm sorry, Tracie. I'm really sorry it turned out this way, and I'm sorry you turned out this way. Maybe someday I can talk to you about true riches."

Even after everything that had happened Davis felt sad watching Chief Hanson and Charley escort the glamorous blond of his youth toward the front door.

She stopped, turned around, grinned showing Davis those little girl dimples that had almost made his knees buckle in past days, and even after all she had done to him, made him feel like a school boy experiencing his first case of love sickness. "Remember what we used to say when we were down late in those high school games? 'It's not over until it's over'."

"I remember us saying that, but I also remember how most of those games ended. It's over Tracie!"

With that she turned walking through the door with the two officers, one on each side of her.

It was Monday. Amy was released from the hospital that morning. She and Jay went out to the new development west of town with a real estate agent to look at a house they were considering purchasing leaving Davis and Deidre together in the girls' apartment. There was work to do, specifically a column that needed to be written, but Davis was in no hurry to get started. Life was simple again and he wanted to savor it.

"What are your plans after Jay and Amy are married? Will you find a new roommate and stay in the apartment?"

"I've been meaning to talk with you about that. If it meets with your approval as landlord I would like to invite Barbara Mason to take Amy's spot when she moves out in August. Barbara was recently widowed. Her husband was my Pastor in South Georgia a few years ago. She is in her early sixties, but is having to return to the classroom due to the recent death of her husband. Her three children are grown and scattered throughout the state. She will be teaching math at Adairsville High School. Barbara is a real character but straight laced, so much so we in the youth group called her *the den mother* when I was a teenager."

"That sounds like a great arrangement. You need a den mother to keep you in line," Davis laughed. "I can hardly wait to meet her.

"Would you be interested in getting a little exercise?" I think I am going to take a walk. Would you like to join me?" Davis asked.

"I would be delighted. Do you think a walk with the landlord could lead to a decrease in rent?"

"You never know!"

They strolled along Railroad Street to College Street. I talked with Mr. Camp, the lawyer from Cape Cod this morning. I guess he has been presented with nothing that would convince him I am Judson Reed's grandson, so if you are being nice to me for my money, you can forget it. I'm as broke as ever, and that isn't likely to change any time soon."

"Isn't that something? Two innocent people dead with others injured for no reason. It is unbelievable how far a person can be driven by greed. Who would doubt the truth of the Bible when it says, "The love of money is the root of all evil?"

"I haven't found the Bible to be wrong about anything yet. I suspect Mr. Brown discovered something beyond what we know, but I guess we will never learn what it was. Tracie seemed absolutely certain that I'm Reed's grandson. That leads me to believe she knows more about it than she lets on. There has been talk of DNA testing, but Reed was cremated and, besides, Tracie would refuse to cooperate."

"Maybe she will eventually break down and confess whatever it is she knows."

"I don't think so. Even though she is never going to be outside a prison again, she is not going to let anyone else have that money."

"It's a shame. You could be on easy street for the rest of your life."

"I guess that would be nice, but it all probably turned out for the best. A lot of money might have robbed me of my motivation. I probably would have ended up a self-indulgent slob."

"I cannot see that happening under any circumstances. Why do you think your mother said nothing in the letter about the identity of her father?"

"I don't know for sure, but my guess is she probably had no knowledge of his identity. It is likely Mary did not divulge that information."

They walked in silence for a time enjoying the beauty of the day. An Adairsville police car passed them. The driver honked his horn and waved. It was Tom, the young policeman Davis had found asleep in the patrol car the morning he captured the "rat faced" man. Davis was glad to see he had not cost the young man his job.

"I think you have an admirer," Davis teased Deidre.

"Oh, I'm the sweetheart of the entire department."

"Is that right?"

"Sure is. Charley invited me to go to the movies with him tonight."

Despite not being able to fight off a surge of jealousy, Davis spoke well of his friend. "He is one of the best men I know. You could do a lot worse than Charley."

"You think so? Then maybe I ought to reconsider. I told him I had a standing Monday night date."

Davis remembered a promise. *"…weeping may remain for a night, but rejoicing comes in the morning."* (Psalm 30:5b) He reached for Deidre's hand. His world was secure again. After finishing their walk, Davis sat down at the computer to write his column. He pecked out his heading:

THE MYSTERY OF DIXIE ADAIR SOLVED!

AFTERWORD

Yes, Adairsville is an actual place and it is nestled in the foothills of North Georgia between Atlanta and Chattanooga. Most of the landmarks described in the story are as presented. Should you visit our little "Norman Rockwell" town you will find across the railroad tracks the big white house with the wrap around porch. It was our home for a time. Our own Corra Harris Bookshop along with the dinner theater is in the 1902 Stock Exchange as described. The Little Rock Café, for many years in the hands of our own families, no longer serves breakfast, but the building, now housing another business, still stands beside the "rock" on the north end of town. The Adairsville Inn continues to prepare some of the best food in North Georgia. The stately little Methodist Church has remained in place with its steeple pointing high toward Heaven. Should you come at the right time of the year you could enjoy the "Great Locomotive Chase Festival" with the thousands of visitors that fill the streets. You would, no doubt, want to ask one of the locals which house Pretty Boy Floyd occupied as a boy, because his childhood was indeed spent in Adairsville, and it is true that he was often seen playing around the depot.

The story of Dixie Adair as found in the prologue is a factual account that came to us through the pen of the late Alice Butler Howard ("Miss Topsy"). Even the names of the participants are the same as in the actual event. The one alteration is that the rescue took place ten years earlier than represented in the prologue. To our knowledge the mystery was never solved. We heard the story, and possible answers to "What if" questions began to formulate. Davis Morgan, Charley Nelson, Deidre, Amy, Tracie and all the others are a result of those questions.

All the characters and events in the story after the prologue are pure fiction; however, should you make that visit to our village, you would meet characters as fascinating as those in the story.

Davis, with the Lord's guidance, the love of family and friends, and Deidre's prayers has begun climbing 'out of the depths', but his journey back is not complete. How will his relationship with Deidre progress? Is there any hope of a permanent arrangement that would include wedding bells? Will Jay and Amy's marriage come off as planned? What about Charley's spiritual life? Can we expect him to come around? Will Davis find his way back to the Ministry or has the Lord permanently led him into the rare book business? These questions along with others are still to be answered in the midst of stimulating new mysteries that will need to be solved. "Miss Helen", the boys from the Little Rock, Janie, Ralph Hayes, Pastor John and a host of new characters will all be there as it unfolds.

Danny & Wanda Pelfrey
Adairsville, Georgia